MAN

W9-BCT-721

Claude Lelouch, *Film Director*

Peter Lev
II

Rutherford ● Madison ● Teaneck
Fairleigh Dickinson University Press
London and Toronto: Associated University Presses

Associated University Presses, Inc.
4 Cornwall Drive
East Brunswick, NJ 08816

Associated University Presses Ltd
27 Chancery Lane
London WC2A 1NF, England

Associated University Presses
Toronto M5E 1A7, Canada

Library of Congress Cataloging in Publication Data

Lev, Peter, 1948–
   Claude Lelouch, film director.

   Filmography: p.
   Bibliography: p.
   Includes index.
   1. Lelouch, Claude, 1937–   2. Moving-picture
producers and directors—France—Biography.   I. Title.
PN1998.A3L4743   791.43′0233′0924 [B] 81-72036
ISBN 0-8386-3114-2   AACR2

Printed in the United States of America

To Yvonne

Contents

Preface

Most people who are interested in European cinema know of Claude Lelouch. He is a very successful film director who has reached large audiences not only in his native France but around the world. He has won several major awards (one Grand Prize at the Cannes Film Festival; two Academy Awards; other prizes in France, Italy, Belgium, Spain, and the United States). Yet serious critical work on Lelouch and his films is extremely sparse. The one book in French, *Claude Lelouch* by Guylaine Guidez (1972), is more notable for its documentation than for its criticism. No other career studies have been done in French or English on Lelouch, so this book is to a large extent breaking new ground.

I became an admirer of Claude Lelouch's work in the early 1970s, when *The Crook, Money, Money, Money, Happy New Year*, and *And Now My Love* appeared, at the rate of about one film per year, on Los Angeles screens. These were extraordinary films that delighted their audiences while evoking almost no critical response. Lelouch had enjoyed his moment of glory some years before, with *A Man and a Woman* (1966), and critics and scholars, even in France, were evidently tired of him. But it seemed to me that Lelouch had gotten considerably better since *A Man and a Woman*. As a UCLA graduate student in cinema, I was fascinated by his combination of humor, romance, and stylistic experiment. In succeeding years, my view of Lelouch has become more nuanced; I am no longer simply a fan. Still, that original fascination is certainly the germ of my book.

The actual research and writing began in 1977. It has taken me to Claude Lelouch's office in Paris, to tiny screening rooms in London and Montreal, to premieres at the Academy of Motion Picture Arts and Sciences, and to dusty newspaper files in library basements. My sincerest thanks to those who helped along the way (see Acknowledgments).

Lelouch is not a favorite of specialized film critics, but there is a considerable body of literature on him and his work. The French daily and weekly press, which considers Lelouch an important director and a celebrity as well, reports on his activities in great detail. This material—interviews, articles, and critical reviews—varies enormously in the quality of both factual reporting and critical judgment. This material is an extremely helpful source for understanding Lelouch, but it must be used with caution. In what follows I have checked all material from the popular press as thoroughly as possible and relied on my own judgment. The many, many published interviews that Lelouch has given pose a special problem, for two reasons. First, Lelouch often has perceptive things to say about his films, but he should not be taken as the last word on them. An artist is never omniscient about his work. Second, Lelouch has given hundreds of interviews, usually to publicize a particular film, so his responses sometimes appear calculated rather than fresh.

The same cautions apply to my own interviews with Lelouch. The first appeared in the Canadian film magazine *Take One*, July–August 1977. The second, previously unpublished, is appended here as a research source that is not otherwise available. Its direct account of a discussion between critic and filmmaker may also provide an interesting counterpoint to the body of this essay.

The question of whether to use the original, foreign-language title of a film or its English translation is always frustrating. I finally decided to use the English translation for films which are well known in the United States; for obscure or unreleased films I use the French title.

Acknowledgments

I would like to thank the many people who generously helped with this project.

In Paris: Claude Lelouch, Tania Zazulinsky, Arlette Gordon, Les Films 13, Editions 23, Michèle Dehaese, Mike and Michele Jerison, Bibliothèque de l'Arsenal, Bibliothèque de l'IDHEC.

In London: Embassy Films.

In Montreal: Pierre Cadieux, Lapointe Films, Criterion Films.

In Los Angeles: Stephen Mamber, Danny Biederman, Howard Suber, Robert Rosen, Marc Bensimon, Charles Speroni, UCLA Film Archives, Charles Hopkins, Narcissa Vanderlip, United Artists, Florence Carpenter, Burt Senkfor, Marc Mancini, Jan Kerwin, and the libraries of California State University Northridge, UCLA, USC, and the Academy of Motion Picture Arts and Sciences.

In New York: Arthur Silverman, United Artists 16.

In Dallas: Paul Monaco, UTD Library, Marsha Rainey, Yvonne and Sara Lev.

Special thanks to the Harold Leonard Foundation and the Nathan and Ida Lev Trust Fund for their financial support of my research.

Introduction

Claude Lelouch is an unusual figure in the recent history of film. He is first of all an accomplished popular filmmaker. He is extremely gifted at putting together images and sounds to communicate with and involve an audience. He works in an entertainment idiom, drawing on genre conventions, the star system, a delight in storytelling, and easily appreciated spectacle. His films center around universal situations and emotions—love, friendship, adventure, laughter, tears—but they also provide a thoughtful view of modern France. Lelouch aims his work at a broad public, and he has become one of the leading popular filmmakers in France. Though not a household name in the United States, he has been fairly successful here with films like *A Man and a Woman* (*Un Homme et une femme*, 1966), *And Now My Love* (*Toute une vie*, 1974), and *Cat and Mouse* (*Le Chat et la souris*, 1975).

On the other hand, Lelouch is part of the movement toward a more personal, more experimental filmmaking that came out of France in the 1950s and 1960s, a movement generally known as the New Wave. He is a leading exponent of the "cinéma d'auteur," the belief that one person should creatively shape a film. As writer, director, producer, and even cameraman of each of his films, Lelouch has a great deal of control over his work. He has used this control to develop certain stylistic and thematic concerns from film to film. Stylistically, his vocabulary is in many ways similar to Godard's. Lelouch intermingles documentary and fictional techniques, makes abrupt jumps in time and space, and comments reflexively on the filmmaking process. Thematically, Lelouch combines the theme of alienation (explored by directors like Godard, Resnais, Antonioni, and Bergman) with more traditional subjects such as love and friendship. His work strives for a kind of synthesis, a unity of modern, critical filmmaking with the traditions of popular art.

Lelouch has been particularly innovative in a technological and organizational sense. His production methods are designed for spontaneity and rapidity. He works very quickly with a small, experienced group of old friends. He hand-holds the camera himself, which gives him greater control of visual style and allows for camera improvisation. He also encourages the actors to improvise, starting from guidelines set by the director. He leaves an important place in his films for the pop-music scores of Francis Lai, which often provide counterpoint to the visual action.

The interest of Lelouch's synthesis can be appreciated in light of recent film history and economics. In the 1950s and 1960s cinema lost the dominant role in popular entertainment it had enjoyed in the previous two decades. Television and other activities (tourism, sports, pop music) took an increasing share of leisure time in the United States and Western Europe. Film no longer reached an extremely broad and diversified public, but instead catered to more specialized groups—for example, young people. This change had both negative and positive consequences. Negatively, the economics of the old commercial cinema broke down; fewer films were made because producers could not depend on a stable and appreciative audience. Positively, the breakdown of the old cinema allowed a place for independent and innovative filmmaking. Europe took the lead here, with such movements as the Art Cinema of the fifties (Fellini, Antonioni, Bergman) and the French New Wave, and American production eventually followed.[1]

Claude Lelouch did not establish the principle that young, educated audiences would come to see ambitious, sophisticated films. He comes after Rossellini, Fellini, Truffaut, Godard, and dozens of others. But there is an important difference between Lelouch and most European directors of note. Filmmakers like Fellini and Godard may start from an appreciation of popular cinema, but their work becomes increasingly intellectual and "artistic" to reflect their interests. Godard, for example, reports that for his first film he wanted to make a realistic gangster picture but was incapable of doing so; he ended up with *Alice in Wonderland* instead of *Scarface*.[2] Godard, the most important filmmaker of his generation, has moved farther and farther away from popular cinema. Lelouch, on the other hand, makes emotionally accessible films for a very broad audience—all the young people who go regularly to films plus some of the older generation who rarely stray from their homes. He tries to use the innovations of the new cinema while still making popular films. Compared to Lelouch, even François Truffaut, who is sometimes called "the filmmaker of the heart," is an intellectual working for elite audiences.

Why insist on the importance of popular cinema in a study obviously devoted, in format and purpose, to serious matters? Because something is lost when film moves away from its popular roots. The popular cinema, with its traditions of genre, the star system, clear storytelling, simple emotions, and moral choices, has the ability to create strong emotional responses and a close bond between film, filmmaker, and audience. It has a tremendous impact, which, admittedly, is often put in the service of trivial or even dangerous ideas. But popular films can also get at the essentials of a situation or an issue because their conventions are so charged with meaning and emotion. They can distill a particular problem—for example, "What is heroism?"—into easily assimilated symbols. A more intellectual cinema may have greater sophistication and perspective, but it will lack this conciseness.

Both of these functions of popular cinema can be seen in Lelouch's films. Their emotional emphasis is brought out by the director's statement that he is interested in only two things, "laughter and tears."[3] Along with fear, these are the most direct emotions a film can transmit to an audience. In his best films, Lelouch is also concerned with cutting through a complicated surface to bring out basic themes like love, friendship, work, and the place of the individual in society. *Money, Money, Money* uses the conventions of the gangster film plus common sense to show the absurdities of contemporary politics, which are contrasted to robust individualism. *A Man and a Woman* and *And Now My Love* cut through a complex modern reality to present the imperatives of love.

Almost all Lelouch films are simple and accessible comedies or melodramas (or both), featuring attractive characters with understandable goals. Lelouch adds to this framework more elaborate thematic and stylistic devices. Visual style expresses a character's feelings or states a general theme. Complex narrative structures connect characters or broaden the significance of a particular event. Allegory and symbolism present a social or political or moral commentary. These are just a few examples of how Lelouch alters his material. Like Godard, he wants "to talk about everything,"[4] to use cinema as a social-personal-emotional art. It is important to note, however, tht Lelouch embellishes popular forms more than he challenges them. His various experiments can be seen as novelties, new twists to old forms. He often has valuable insights, but he does not contradict the accessibility, good humor, and common sense of popular cinema.

In studies of film directors it has been fashionable for many years to glorify or (more infrequently) vilify the subject under consideration. Both of these approaches offer easy logic, a clear statement of values, and the opportunity to polemicize. But it should be obvious that adulation or attack often greatly simplifies a filmmaker's work. Like all of us, film directors struggle, experiment, and make mistakes, and a responsible criticism should recognize this while also appreciating a director's accomplishments. A criticism that examines both the failures and the beauties of a work lacks the polemical flair of adulation or attack, but I think it is the most intellectually honest approach. I have attempted that kind of balanced criticism in this study of Lelouch.

Lelouch's record as a popular and aesthetic-intellectual-critical filmmaker is very partial and uneven. He has flaws as a director, and he will not be put on a pedestal here. His films are frequently disorganized, particularly when the different levels of experiment do not mesh. *Live for Life*, for example, is a film of marvelous parts whose visual style, music, acting, story, and social theme just do not fit together. Lelouch's emphasis on very simple themes and emotions can distort his view of a problem. *The Good and the Bad*, a film on the German Occupation of France, suffers from a cops-and-robbers tone imposed on a serious subject. And Lelouch's interest in improvisation and taking risks can lead to failures of structure and content. He is certainly an ambitious filmmaker, but he rarely, if ever, realizes his ambitions.

Lelouch's achievement can be appreciated, though, if we consider what he is trying to do. It is extremely difficult to have new ideas *and* communicate them so lucidly and effectively that a large audience can understand and follow them. This kind of filmmaking reaches out to both the intellect and the emotions; it requires a mixture of what James Monaco (writing about other New Wave directors) calls "Method" and "Sentiment."[5] Lelouch is at least trying to combine entertainment and reflection, and his career suggests that filmmakers can work between these two poles without becoming uncommercial. At his best, Lelouch appeals to the spectator on multiple levels. He communicates everything from the most fugitive impressions to the most basic emotions, from clever asides to complex intellectual and artistic structures. At his worst, Lelouch is still amusing, technically innovative, and capable of occasional brilliant moments.

This book provides a study of Lelouch's attempted synthesis through five major phases. First, in the period before *A Man and a Woman*, he is a precocious, brash, and often incoherent filmmaker. His films are entertaining and full of ideas but thoroughly undisciplined. Second, the four films from *A Man and a Woman* (1966) through *Un Homme qui me plaît* (1969) show Lelouch developing a subjective style that suggests feelings through film technique. He follows the immense success of *A Man and a Woman*, a very simple subject presented with great subtlety, by applying the same style to more ambitious themes. Third, in the films from *The Crook* (1970) to *Happy New Year* (1973) Lelouch works within a single genre, the crime film. This is his most successful period, because the genre form disciplines his filmmaking while allowing for two or more levels of meaning. After the unique and ambitious *And Now My Love* (1974), Lelouch's fourth major period stretches from *Le Mariage* (1974) to *Another Man, Another Chance* (1977). These films combine some explicit moralizing with light genre entertainment. Since *Another Man, Another Chance*, Lelouch has directed *Robert et Robert* (1978), *A nous deux* (1979), and *The Ins and the Outs* (1981). The three films of his latest period are diverse (comedy, crime film, epic) but closely linked to his previous work.

The book discusses individual films in detail, because particulars are very important in Lelouch's films. An overly abstract view would obscure the originality of his techniques and structures. The description of each film covers the plot, the major stylistic qualities, and the way critical-experimental and traditional-popular elements are combined in an overall structure. Additional information on Lelouch's biography, production conditions, film history and aesthetics, and social and political history is included as it illuminates his artistic choices. The development of Lelouch's cinema—relationships between films, changes in goals and methods—is also discussed at length. The overall aim is to analyze and evaluate Lelouch's mix of critical-experimental and popular filmmaking through a detailed career study.

After the discussion of individual films, two chapters connect Lelouch to his contemporaries in the French New Wave, first in stylistic and then in thematic terms. This may not be the only way to put his work in artistic context. However, these chapters do show that Lelouch has many things in common with the New Wave. He has made a particular response to questions posed by a large group of filmmakers.

Claude Lelouch, *Film Director*

1
Beginnings

Claude Lelouch was born on October 30, 1937, in the Strasbourg–Saint-Denis neighborhood of Paris. His father owned a small business in the area. Lelouch's parents were Jews who had emigrated to France from Algeria. During World War II M. Lelouch returned to Algeria, but young Claude and his mother were stranded in France where they spent four years hiding from the Nazis. Lelouch suggests that his experiences during this period are the basis of his self-reliance and his love of individual freedom.[1]

Soon after the war Lelouch became a devoted moviegoer. He spent hours every day watching genre films (Westerns, adventure films, gangster films, erotic films) at the many theaters in his neighborhood.[2] He was most interested in American films, which had triumphantly returned to Paris after being banned under the German Occupation. Then, as a young teenager, Lelouch began going regularly to screenings at Henri Langlois's Cinémathèque Française, which provided an extremely thorough and varied introduction to cinematic culture for Lelouch and many other filmmakers and critics of postwar France. Lelouch has, however, retained more affection for the genre films of his childhood than for the masterpieces of the Cinémathèque.

Unlike many of the "children of the Cinémathèque," Lelouch is not a well-educated intellectual with a passion for cinema. He is, instead, a self-taught, self-made man. He had very little formal schooling, attending a number of lycées without graduating, and he picked up a knowledge of cinema independent of other cultural pursuits. Lelouch says: "I started reading at the age of twenty-five. . . . Before the age of twenty-five, only cinema interested me. All I saw was films, films, films, films and television."[3] Even today, Lelouch has much more confidence in his own experiences and his knowledge of films than in literature or abstract thinking.

Lelouch started making films at the age of fourteen with an eight-millimeter camera. One of his early films, *Le Mal du siècle*, won the grand prize at an amateur festival in 1954. Guidez describes it as "a parable about war presented through the games at a country fair."[4] After Lelouch failed the baccalaureate exam, his father gave him a sixteen-millimeter camera, and he quickly became a free-lance news camera-man. His first films were *USA en vrac* (an unflattering montage of a trip through the United States) and *Une Ville pas comme les autres* (a pictur-esque view of New York). Lelouch next went to the Soviet Union, where he filmed secretly with a camera under his coat; he was even able to shoot some footage in Lenin's tomb. This film, *Quand le rideau se lève*, was bought by American television for $20,000.

In 1956, Lelouch, at the age of eighteen, covered the Suez invasion, the Hungarian revolution, and other major stories as a free-lance news cameraman. He sold his film reports to European and American televi-sion networks on his return to Paris. Television news was a small opera-tion at this time, with reporters in only a few important centers. For other stories, TV networks depended on newsreel companies and free-lancers. So, there was room for enterprising cameramen to cover even the biggest news stories.

Lelouch's career as a news cameraman cannot have lasted long, for from 1957 to 1960 he was in the army, working for the Service Cinématographique des Armées. He directed a number of instructional films in both sixteen and thirty-five millimeter. One of these, *La Guerre du silence*, was a story film that gave him a chance to direct actors.

No one would hire Lelouch as a film director when he got out of the army, so he founded his own production company, Les Films 13, and made his first feature film, *Le Propre de l'homme*. The film was made by a small group of his friends, without union authorization, on the streets of Paris. The minimal budget for the film came from Lelouch's savings plus everything he could borrow. The story is about a young couple who spend a day and a night wandering through Paris and getting to know each other. Lelouch himself and Janine Magnan, his girl friend, produc-tion assistant, and lead actress during the early 1960s, play the main roles. The black-and-white film concludes with a passage of abstract images in color accompanied by sound effects suggesting the future of the couple (marriage, birth of a baby, war, peace).

Le Propre de l'homme begins with a long introductory title that ex-plicitly limits its subject matter, stating that no serious problem is dis-cussed except perhaps the beauty of a twenty-year-old's smile. Unfortunately, the film has trouble sustaining its slim premise of boy meets girl. The first few minutes of the film present several amusing gags about girl chasing, including the title appearing over a young lady's rear end. The body of the film, though, is a much looser journey through Paris, with lots of candid camera scenes and a very understated story. The idea of expressing a love story through documentary views of a city has impressive antecedents (city symphony films like *Rien que les heures*, surrealist prose poems like *Nadja*, many different kinds of novels), but in this film the documentary footage only occasionally adds to the fictional story. Therefore, the film is very slow; a day stretches on forever. Other problems in the film include dialogue that is almost unintelligible and a shy, uncertain acting performance by Lelouch.

The film does have a few glimmers of Lelouch's future style. Some scenes are visually exciting—long tracking shots at the beginning of boys following girls, a lyrical car ride anticipating *A Man and a Woman*, an expressionistic shot of the hotel where the couple finishes the evening. *Le Propre de l'homme* also has a little of the variety of Lelouch's later work—it mixes documentary and fiction, ends with a shift to color, and uses several kinds of musical accompaniment. Still, it is very much a tentative first effort.

Le Propre de l'homme was made in the middle of the New Wave period, when dozens of young directors, many with documentary experience, were making experimental, low-budget features. Some of these directors achieved stunning success, but Lelouch's film attracted no great interest. It played briefly at a Paris Art and Essay theater, got mediocre reviews, and did almost no business. One of the few positive results of the film was an encouraging phone call to Lelouch from Pierre Braunberger, the veteran producer who had worked with Jean Renoir in the early 1930s and was now producing films like *Moi un Noir* (Jean Rouch, 1959), *Tirez sur le pianiste* (François Truffaut, 1960), *Un Coeur gros comme ça* (François Reichenbach, 1961) and *Vivre sa vie* (Jean-Luc Godard, 1962). Braunberger's company, Les Films de la Pléiade, was to be coproducer of all of Lelouch's feature films through *A Man and a Woman* (1966).

After *Le Propre de l'homme* Lelouch got a lucky break. His major creditor, Eclair Laboratories, found him a job working on a new audio-visual product, the Scopitone.[5] This was a kind of jukebox with images that played three-minute color films, shown on a twenty-one-inch screen. The films featured France's leading pop singers (Johnny Hallyday, Sylvie Vartan, Françoise Hardy and others) performing their latest hits. Scopitone directors had a great deal of leeway in choosing the situations or stories of their films; the major requirement was an ability to work rapidly and cheaply.

Lelouch soon became the leading director of Scopitones. Where the first Scopitones had been shot straightforwardly on one set, Lelouch's three-minute films were made in real exteriors with dancers, changing backgrounds, and inventive uses of color. Holding the camera himself, Lelouch was able to work very quickly and still create elaborate stylistic effects. He developed a visual style of flamboyant zooms,* tracks, and cuts to match the energy of the yé-yé songs. All contemporary accounts

---

*The zoom is an obtrusive visual technique that often calls attention to itself at the expense of the subject. However, it fits Lelouch's dynamic, extroverted style very well. He has been known for his zooms since the early 1960s.

agree on the inventiveness, the technical facility, and the skillful melding of images and sounds in Lelouch's Scopitones; Robert Benayoun even compares them to the best American musical comedies.[6]

The Scopitone had a strong influence on Lelouch's career. Without this experience, Lelouch may not have so thoroughly mastered the striking visual style and the unique use of pop music which characterize his later feature films. Many of the musical interludes in Lelouch's films are Scopitone-like, and he has used a number of pop-music stars as actors and singers. The Scopitone also imposed a kind of professional discipline on Lelouch, since it required brief, efficient, and entertaining filmmaking. Still, one should not overemphasize the artistic possibilities of the form. Though Lelouch says that making Scopitones was "amusing,"[7] he filmed a few hundred of them in the early 1960s mainly as a way to pay his debts and support more ambitious projects. He also made numerous commercials (for television and movie theaters) at this time for the same reasons.

Lelouch's next feature film, *L'Amour avec des si*, was made in 1962. It tells the story of a man, played by Guy Mairesse, driving through the Northwest of France on a midwinter vacation. Intercut with his trip are radio reports (accompanied by filmed visualizations) about a notorious rapist who has escaped from prison, as well as other news and entertainment programs. Cutting, acting, the rapist's description, and the atmosphere of violence created by the news all suggest that our traveler is the rapist. Thus, when he picks up a pretty hitchhiker (Janine Magnan), we fear for her safety. Eventually the police start chasing the couple, confirming our suspicions. But at the film's denouement it turns out that the hitchhiker is the criminal; she has a long history of seducing tourists, feeding them knockout drops, and then stealing their money. A subsequent scene of the rapist being caught in another part of France removes any lingering doubts about the hero.

At one level, the film is about the dangers of publicity. Lelouch shows how a collective obsession can be created and carried by the media. Without the radio and supporting visual cues we would have a far different view of the story. Lelouch further suggests that the media can push people into irrational actions. In one scene Janine Magnan, parked on the coast near the ruins of a German battlement, reacts so strongly to a radio documentary about World War II that she runs out screaming into the night. Lelouch includes a scary but obtrusive visualization of a battle here to illustrate the broadcast's powers of suggestion. We also expect Guy Mairesse to react violently to the violent tension built up by radio reports on the rapist. This never happens, but Magnan's temporary loss of control indicates that it *could* happen.

The film's other central focus, the "courtship" of Magnan and

Mairesse, also involves media trickery. The film proposes two interpretations of this couple: first, that Mairesse may be the rapist; second, that a chance affair on vacation is a simple, natural thing. The second interpretation is suggested by the flirting of the two main characters in the context of a "movie romance." It is echoed by an extremely simple love song that recurs several times, a love song which says little more than "I love you, you love me." Both these interpretations turn out to be incorrect, because Lelouch has misled the audience and Mairesse has perhaps misled himself. The film ends with a more complex song telling how the hero committed himself despite his doubts (*L'Amour avec des si* can be translated as "Love with Doubts"), but found himself alone.

L'Amour avec des si could have been a very pessimistic film about how the media are distorting people's lives. However, although the film takes place in the bleakest winter landscape, its potential seriousness is undercut by a lively, comic tone. Some of the comic situations are fairly standard—the inept policemen, the miserly innkeeper who gives away his finest delicacies in trying to retain the suspects. More interesting, though, is an anarchic, youthful wit that is largely lacking in Lelouch's later films. Lelouch makes fun in this film of the church and the army, stages a drag race cut to the idiotic love song, and punctuates the film with loud music, violent changes of mood, and extravagant zooms and tracks. The film also introduces a uniquely insolent female character: Janine Magnan blithely declares that rape is a female invention and later performs a kind of mating dance in her corset, a portable radio in hand. The film's brashness and good spirits make it more a comic misadventure than a serious critique of the mass media.

Although it overflows with ideas, *L'Amour avec des si*'s mixture of genres is not very successful in execution. Its many twists and turns finally become tiresome, because we know we are being manipulated. Lelouch has particular trouble with the Guy Mairesse character, who is supposed to be at the same time a world-weary traveler, an innocent young lover, and a possible rapist. The film also has some of the problems one would expect in a very low-budget, experimental film: poor sound quality, difficulties with pacing, awkward inserts. Lelouch does not yet have the stylistic control that is needed to bring off his ambitious design.

One device that does work very well in the film is the use of Gérard Sire as the news announcer. Sire, a well-known personality on French radio and television, has the authoritative and highly personal delivery of a media professional. The continual use of his voice gives the radio an insinuating, all-permeating quality. Sire plays the spokesman of the mass media in several of Lelouch's films.

L'Amour avec des si, like *Le Propre de l'homme*, was a commercial failure. It played a few engagements abroad, but was not released in France until 1965. After making the film, Lelouch returned to directing Scopitones and commercials.

In 1963, Lelouch made *La Femme Spectacle*, a feature-length mixture of documentary scenes and fictional sketches that was suggested by Pierre Braunberger. It was a study of the women of Paris in their more spectacular aspects, from the birth of a baby to a striptease act. Both Lelouch and Braunberger seem to have considered the film an exploitation documentary, a purely money-making proposition. However, the film was badly mangled by the French censors, who required forty-five minutes of cuts. It was never released in any form in France, but it was exported in its shortened version. The film was shown in a dubbed, shortened version in England under the title *Paris in the Raw*.

What remains of *La Femme Spectacle* is far from inspiring. A few scenes do have either immediate shock value (a nose job shown in horrifying detail) or an interesting thematic point (a long interview with female impersonators exploring the theme of appearance and reality). However, other scenes are simply ludicrous: transparently faked "cinéma-vérité" interviews, a miserably written and acted sketch about divorce, a silly sketch about a soldier confusing a real masseuse with a prostitute. The dialogue for the film is very bad, and even Lelouch's visual technique sometimes fails him (sample montage: zoom in on the masseuse's address; zoom in on the soldier looking for the address). The worst thing about the film, though, is a long-winded commentary full of pseudo-philosophy and classical references. This thin veneer of "culture" (probably for the censors' benefit) is one of the most ridiculous conventions of the exploitation documentary.

Lelouch now says that *La Femme Spectacle* is a "horrible, horrible" film. He adds that Pierre Braunberger was primarily responsible for its idea, script, and production.[8]

Une Fille et des fusils, made in 1964, was the first Lelouch film produced in normal film industry conditions, with government and union authorizations. The story follows the adventures of four young factory workers—Jean-Pierre (Jean-Pierre Kalfon), Jacques (Jacques Portet), Pierre (Pierre Barouh), and Amidou (Amidou). Frustrated by their daily lives and inspired by the movies, the four decide to become criminals. They are joined by Jacques's deaf-mute girl friend Martine (Janine Magnan), whose handicap may symbolize an incompleteness in all of their lives. After a period of self-instruction and petty theft, the novice gangsters kidnap a sexy movie star—they actually end up with her stand-in—and demand a huge ransom. Their plan goes awry, resulting in the murder of several innocent bystanders on the Champs Elysées. Shocked and remorseful, the four protagonists kill each other in a movie-style "shootout."

Like *L'Amour avec des si, Une Fille et des fusils* is more a comic study of mass media than a realistic crime story. In this case, the subject is movie fantasies and their influence on daily life. The film begins with a parody of gangster movies and never strays far from movie themes. At various points in the film, the heroes try to emulate John Wayne and James Stewart, plan their strategy based on movie models, and debate whether gangster films need to end badly. A bombastic musical theme by Pierre Vassiliu, based on the music for American Westerns, also plays with ideas of movie heroism. The theme is often used ironically, as in a scene where the four heroes elaborately steal a pack of gum.

Lelouch's gags about movies become especially interesting when they involve an interplay between media fantasy and real life. In one sequence, for example, the would-be gangsters challenge a neighborhood gang called "la bande de Williams." The challenge, delivered by spilled drinks and a cigarette put out in a coffee cup, is hilarious, but it is also a fair representation of how movie ideas of honor show up, often distorted, in everyday life. The film's commentary adds a further insight to the scene by noting, after a particularly daring act, that "Amidou later admitted he was afraid." This kind of detail adds depth to characters who might otherwise be stereotyped.

The film has considerable difficulty making the delicate transition from comedy to tragedy. First, the exchange of the starlet on the Champs Elysées is filmed in a scattered, offhand way that lessens its impact. Perhaps Lelouch lacked either the resources or the experience to shoot a big action scene here. Then, the final shootout is presented in a very exaggerated way (bizarre camera angles, acrobatic camera movements, athletic acting), and the heroes' sudden deaths are extremely jarring after the exuberance of most of the film. The ending is so depressing, in fact, that Lelouch added a scene for the film's American distributor, showing the main characters waking up on a beach after the shootout.[9]

The original French ending was so unconvincing that some critics assumed it was concocted purely to satisfy the censors, and that Lelouch would have preferred to let his characters go free.[10] Lelouch, however, says that the French version has the ending he wanted.[11] In this film, as in many of his other films, Lelouch is trying for a mixture of genres that will expand the audience's conventional emotional responses. The mix of moods shows a commitment to realism not in each detail, but in the sense that even the giddiest adventure can have real, serious consequences. The film thus needs something to indicate the magnitude of what went wrong, and the heroes' dawning realization of their guilt. But having the heroes wipe each other out is an incoherent way to deal with the moral problem.

Une Fille et des fusils' most striking attribute is its half-parodic, half-serious tone. The film works on several levels—as a series of gags, an homage to the action film, a commentary on the effects of movies, a story about working-class youth. Lelouch enhances the film's multileveled quality by making each episode semiautonomous, depending for continuity on thematic connections and consistency of tone as well as a basic story line. Some of the episodes are truly outrageous—a fantasy sequence of the heroes in western garb, a scene in which Amidou forces the starlet to strip (thus realizing the dream of a movie spectator). Other, quieter sequences show the heroes at work in the Simca factory, sitting in their favorite café, or wandering through the city. By working between parody or fantasy and reality, the film gains a tremendous liberty of expression.

Although the overall tone of the film is very attractive, some rough spots do remain. The prominent subplot about Martine and Jacques, including a long walking scene reminiscent of *Le Propre de l'homme*, mainly slows the film down. Their nonverbal love affair is not strong enough to balance the comic adventure plot. Gérard Sire's commentary adds a reflective dimension, but the form of the commentary is obtrusive and irritating—he is supposedly a reporter dictating to his secretary, and his speeches are accompanied by the sound of a typewriter. Fighting scenes, including the final shootout, are so exaggerated that they sometimes resemble tumbling exhibitions. Lelouch is still having trouble in making all his ideas cohere.

After *Une Fille et des fusils* Lelouch was naturally compared to Jean-Luc Godard, the controversial director who had pioneered the half-parodic, self-reflexive, collage style. Lelouch's film has much of the humor, the collage approach, and the thematic density of Godard's early work. There are even specific points of contact—the starlet's strip resembles a famous scene in *Les Carabiniers* (1963), and the plot of *Une Fille et des fusils* is very similar to that of Godard's *Bande à part* (both films were made in 1964; *Bande à part* was released at about the same time that Lelouch's film was being shot). Although there may be an influence here, it seems more important to note that Lelouch has mastered much of the Godardian idiom while maintaining a unique personality of his own. Lelouch is a less self-conscious and more extroverted filmmaker than Godard. His *Une Fille et des fusils* may be less sophisticated than Godard's *Bande à part*, but both are impressive films.

Une Fille et des Fusils was a big success at film festivals and had a modest commercial career. It won prizes at the first Festival of Young Cinema at Hyères and the Mar del Plata Festival. After a fairly good Paris opening, where it was advertised as "a French *Rebel without a Cause*," the film was distributed throughout France and in many foreign countries. It also received a good deal of critical attention and established Lelouch's credibility in the French film industry.

The next Lelouch film, *Les Grands Moments*, was a comedy-gangster film in Scope featuring the same cast as *Une fille et des fusils*. The plot of *Les Grands Moments* involves four imprisoned gangsters (older, more experienced criminals than in the earlier film) who are commissioned by the police to build an invincible armored truck. Released from prison after the truck passes various tests, the four gangsters then attack it themselves. However, the authorities have been counting on this reaction as a final test for the vehicle; the four are captured and sent back to jail. The convoluted plot, with its accent on outwitting one's adversaries, anticipates later Lelouch films, especially *Money, Money, Money (L'Aventure c'est l'aventure*, 1972).

Les Grands Moments was not released in 1965, for reasons which remain unknown, and Lelouch has since decided not to show it at all. He now feels that the film was a failure. Since I have not been able to see it, I will not comment further.

Lelouch stopped making Scopitones and commercials after *Une Fille et des fusils*, but he did direct a few documentaries and an occasional television show in the mid-1960's. The most important of the documentaries was *Pour un maillot jaune* (1965), an impressionistic study of the Tour de France bicycle race. The film is about the whole environment surrounding a major sporting event—spectators, media coverage, musicians, ceremonies, vehicles of every description, and, of course, the cyclists. It is to some extent analogous to the films about media distortion, since the Tour de France is a media and advertising circus as well as a race. Lelouch is not trying to make a point, though, but merely showing the chaos and spectacle of the event. These qualities are emphasized by fast cutting, a constantly moving camera, and a sound track with lots of noise and music but very few words. The most interesting technical device in the film is the monochrome tinting of many scenes. The tinted scenes, alternating with normal color, provide some structure and variation for a subject that could easily become boring. However, *Pour un maillot jaune* is still a rather jerky and repetitive film.

Claude Lelouch's early career was strongly marked by his very broad experience in different kinds of filmmaking. He had a unique, and unplanned, apprenticeship in various marginal areas of film production: amateur filmmaking, news free-lancing, documentaries, Scopitones, commercials, and films for television. Lelouch learned from these experiences both the basics of film technique and the specific vocabularies of the forms he worked in. Much of his distinctive feature film style has roots in his early work: the hand-held camera in amateur filmmaking and news reporting; the zoom in reporting, Scopitones, and commercials; the contrapuntal use of pop music in Scopitones. Lelouch also learned a good deal about how the media interact with audiences, and this influenced both the content and the style of his later feature films.

A fascinating aspect of Lelouch's apprenticeship in movies is that many of the forms he worked in had not even existed a few years earlier; they were part of the explosion of audio-visual media in the post–World War II period. The mixture of genres, tones, and styles that is such an important part of Lelouch's work may very well be a response to working and living in a world crowded with media. Lelouch likes to say that he belongs to the generation of the image, the generation that was brought up on film and television, and thus he sees things differently than older directors do.

As a director of feature films, Lelouch very quickly developed a complicated style of surprises, shifts in tone, and multiple themes. His best films of the early 1960s, *L'Amour avec des si* and *Une Fille et des fusils*, are an exciting mixture of genre parody with perceptive observations of the contemporary world. However, Lelouch's taste for complication sometimes leads him to incoherence, and his broadly comic scenes are much better than his attempts to deal with other themes and emotions. Even *Une Fille et des fusils* only sketchily and awkwardly indicates an ambitious thematic design behind a playful surface. Lelouch at this time combines a fine sense of the implications of film style with the immaturity of a very young filmmaker.

2
Subjectivity

A Man and a Woman (*Un Homme et une femme*, 1966)

After the failure of *Les Grands Moments*, Lelouch immediately began work on *A Man and a Woman*. The film was budgeted at a modest $100,000, but since he was already seriously in debt, even this relatively small amount was difficult for him to raise. Starting money came from $14,000 cash plus an "avance sur recettes" from the French government.[1] While he was shooting *A Man and a Woman*, Lelouch was able to sell American distribution rights to Allied Artists for $40,000, which allowed him to finish the film. Ford-France also contributed greatly by loaning the production three Ford Mustangs and four racing cars.[2]

Jean-Louis Trintignant and Anouk Aimée, the first well-known actors in Lelouch's films, were recruited for the film because Trintignant had admired *Une Fille et des fusils*. Trintignant agreed to play the male lead and helped Lelouch get Aimée (a close friend of Nadine Trintignant's) for the other main role. Actually, although they had worked in the movie industry for many years, Trintignant and Aimée were not major stars until they acted in *A Man and a Woman*. The boy and girl in the film were the children of Lelouch's friends Gérard Sire and Amidou.

The film was shot cheaply and efficiently in three weeks with a crew of five. Almost everything was shot on location (some of the closeups in the car may have been mocked up in a studio). Anouk Aimée describes the production conditions as follows:

> Jean-Louis and I not only did our own makeup and attended to our own wardrobe but we also helped with the lights. We had no sets. For a scene on the train from Deauville to Paris, Lelouch and I actually took the train to Paris and he filmed en route. For the rest, the company traveled over half of France in only two automobiles, and to save hotel and meal expenses we worked on Saturdays and Sundays.[3]

Many of the film's unique stylistic qualities can be partially explained by the conditions in which it was made. For example, the film was shot

31

partly in color to satisfy the American distributor, who was thinking
about an eventual television sale. However, night scenes and interiors
were shot in black-and-white to save money. Later, Lelouch had the
black-and-white footage printed in different monochrome tones (blue,
orange, green, sepia). He had already used this technique in *Pour un
maillot jaune* to give some variation to a bicycle race. In *A Man and a
Woman* the monochrome sequences not only provide variations for editing but also indicate changes of mood and distinctions between past and
present. François Chevassu notes other money-saving techniques in the
film—avoidance of synchronized sound, music or noise instead of dialogue, panning shots with a telephoto lens instead of complex camera
movements.[4] The key point about these techniques, though, is not what
inspired them but how well they work in the film.

Jean-Louis Duroc (Jean-Louis Trintignant) visits his son Antoine (Antoine Sire) every weekend at a boarding school in Deauville. Anne
Gautier (Anouk Aimée) visists her daughter Françoise (Souad Amidou)
every weekend at the same school. The schoolmistress introduces Jean-
Louis and Anne one Sunday evening after Anne has missed her train
back to Paris, and Jean-Louis drives her back. During the ride Anne
describes her husband Pierre (Pierre Barouh) in a series of flashbacks—
his work as a movie stuntman, his wonderful qualities, and, finally, his
accidental death. The following scene shows Jean-Louis at work test-
driving race cars. On the next Sunday Jean-Louis and Anne drive together to Deauville and take their children out for lunch and a boat ride.
On the way home Jean-Louis describes, in flashback, the suicide of his
wife, who thought he was critically injured in a racing accident. A few
days later Jean-Louis competes in the Monte Carlo Rally and wins.
Anne sends him a telegram: "Bravo. I love you."

After receiving the telegram, Jean-Louis immediately drives from
Monte Carlo to Paris, but finds that Anne is at Deauville. He continues
on to Deauville where he finds Anne with the children on the beach.
Anne and Jean-Louis drop off the children at school and then make love
in a hotel room. But Anne is troubled by memories of her husband,
shown in flashback, and she becomes frigid. Jean-Louis puts her on a
train to Paris, then decides to follow her by car. He is there waiting
when Anne's train arrives. They embrace.

A Man and a Woman is a curious film, half sophisticated, half naive.
There is nothing unusual about the story—a young woman is pulled
between an attractive man and the memories and obligations of her
past. Lelouch has put this subject into a fluid and exciting modern
idiom, but he has also given it extremely melodramatic qualities—
perfect characters, strong emotions, a glamorous world. The results of
this synthesis can be breathtaking when Lelouch's style adds nuance
and feeling to a situation, but they can also be awkward and simplistic.

A Man and a Woman—Jean-Louis Trintignant. (Allied Artists)

A dynamic, forceful, and direct visual style makes *A Man and a Woman* something more than an ordinary love story. Drawing on his experience in making Scopitones and commericals, Lelouch uses angle, lens choice, symbolism, movement, and editing to provide maximum impact for every moment of the film. Rapid, elliptical cutting barrages the spectator with images and creates a pattern of surprises. The use of color (for the first time in a Lelouch feature) adds a new, lyrical dimension. Some critics have seen echoes of Godard (shock cutting), Resnais (ellipses of time and space), and Antonioni (moody, evocative landscapes) in the film. Lelouch also uses documentary techniques to give the film conviction and vigor. His hand-held camera intimately explores the characters' behavior, while, by shooting in real locations, often with available light, he creates a sense of interaction between the fictional story and the real world.

This eclectic style is more controlled here than in his earlier films. Lelouch does occasionally linger over picturesque images and spectacular camera movements; he likes shots of sunset, sunrise, automobile racing, and a dog running on the beach. Still, where in *Une Fille et des fusils* each action scene was an excuse for fanciful camera acrobatics, in *A Man and a Woman* everything is subordinated to the overall emotional effect. Even the famous Lelouch zoom is used sparingly and well.

The film's most important stylistic innovation is the extensive use of montage sequences. Many key scenes are shown by a series of striking images cut to music, with dialogue and narrative continuity replaced by the meanings of the image-sound combinations. This technique allows Lelouch to present information quickly and evocatively, instead of working through narrative expositon. It also sets up a structure of contrasts (of content, visual style, color, music) between sequences. Even the more conventionally edited scenes become part of the pattern of variations.

The montages are extremely varied in function and tone. Anne's flashbacks, for example, are idyllic memories of her husband, presented in a few fleeting images. The color flashbacks, erupting from a blue-tinted night scene, suggest that Anne is more alive in the past than in the present. Lelouch shows us Jean-Louis's profession, rather than telling us about it, in a documentarylike sequence of test-driving. This sets up another sequence in which we see Jean-Louis's fanciful description of himself as a pimp. The growing connection between Anne and Jean-Louis is shown by two sequences of parallel editing—first, Jean-Louis racing and Anne working or relaxing; then, Jean-Louis in his car and Anne on the train, the individual shots getting shorter and shorter until they almost merge, anticipating the film's happy ending.

The music by Lai and Barouh supports the film's changing moods while adding original elements of its own. Early in the film, music is used only sparingly. Barouh's samba (one of Anne's flashbacks) shows what a wonderful guy Pierre was, while a percussive theme accompanies the scenes of Jean-Louis's test-driving and racing. At the end of the film, song follows song as Lelouch and Lai build to a climax. The love song "Aujourd'hui c'est toi," accompanying the first parallel montage, cements the connection between Anne and Jean-Louis.* The film's theme plays under Jean-Louis's drive to Paris. "A l'ombre de nous," a symbolist dirge, breaks the euphoric mood as Anne recalls her husband while she is in bed with Jean-Louis. "L'amour est bien plus fort que nous" restores hope, although the images (Anne and Jean-Louis parting) are sad and reserved. The film ends with the sentimental theme song. This "musical" construction of images and sounds, which Lelouch also uses in *And Now My Love* and *The Good and the Bad*, brings the film to a powerful conclusion.

Lelouch's extensive use of montage has both strengths and weaknesses. The fleeting, fragmented images nicely express an uncertain relationship, and they allow the spectator to read his or her own hopes and fears into the characters. Lelouch is actually able to suggest something of how it feels to be in love. The interconnections of past and

---

*The racing theme is a variation on "Aujourd'hui c'est toi," which suggests that Jean-Louis' profession has a sexual attraction.

present, the empathy with nature, the violent clash of moods, the emotional tone of each moment all work toward this effect. However, there is also a kind of thinness in the film's montage approach. Secondary characters are not developed, plot is subordinated to montage, flashy images and movements produce predictable emotional responses. Further, the montage sometimes seems only to approximate the content of a scene. Barouh's samba, accompanied by images of horseback riding in Camargue, presents only a vague, confused lyricism, and Lelouch does not find the powerful memory images that will make Anne's frigidity meaningful.

Lelouch's approach in the film could be called subjective filmmaking. Although the images are not seen from one character's point of view ("subjective camera"), the film does powerfully present the moods and feelings of the main characters. Montage, music, color, and camera movement all come together to express what Jean-Louis and Anne are feeling. Apparently realistic and objective scenes are thus "invaded" by a strong emotional tone. Subjective filmmaking requires a great deal of subtlety and sophistication, since every detail must work to achieve the desired emotional effect while avoiding cliché. Further, the highly charged scenes must be woven into an integrated whole. Lelouch manages this fairly well, although his lyrical, evocative images are sometimes undisciplined (the samba scene) or clichéd (the dog on the beach).

The film's central character relationship is fairly straightforward. Lelouch describes *A Man and a Woman* as the story of a "privileged moment"; Jean-Louis and Anne, both in their early thirties, meet at exactly the moment when their past experience is balanced by a sense of continuing possibility.[5] So, we have two characters very lucidly but also emotionally exploring a new relationship. The particular tone of this moment is set by the shyness and vulnerability of both characters. Their meeting is full of false starts and feigned nonchalance, but it also has an understated passion and intensity. The flashbacks and other montages suggest the hidden depths of the relationship.

The characters and acting of *A Man and a Woman* can be illuminated by some discussion of Lelouch's direction of actors. His method, which has not drastically changed in twenty years, involves a controlled spontaneity. The actors never see a script, and Lelouch never tells them the complete plot. Instead, before each scene, he gives some partial indications of dialogue and action. Often one actor does not know what another will do, so, starting from the director's instructions, they react to each other and work out a scene. The hand-held camera follows the action. Lelouch explains:

They (the actors) discover the film every day as it is being shot. This doesn't give them a chance to do their number, to be actors. They

A Man and a Woman—Anouk Aimée. (Allied Artists)

remain human beings who are afraid, let's say, of what happens to them.[6]

This method is not complete improvisation because Lelouch thoroughly prepares both the script and the technical aspects of the film. Actors and camera elaborate on a basic outline. The director remains in charge, but he gives the actors a degree of creative autonomy.

Trintignant and Aimée give excellent performances within this framework. They create emotionally persuasive characters even in the most fragmented scenes. Because of Lelouch's shooting methods the actors have to "live" their parts, having confidence in their own reactions and the camera's ability to capture them. The actors are aided by roles that are close to their own personalities and abilities. Trintignant comes from a family of racing drivers, and he suggested to Lelouch that his character should be a driver rather than a lawyer or a doctor.[7] He is charming and relaxed behind the wheel, but he is also good at playing sensitive, uncertain characters (as in Eric Rohmer's *My Night at Maud's*, 1969). Aimée has a proud and serious but very vulnerable beauty. She is evidently shy and fearful in her personal life, and the film plays on this quality.[8] Lelouch often shows her head slightly tilted or in profile, giving her a questioning, unsure look. Both actors have a combi-

A Man and a Woman—Anouk Aimée and Pierre Barouh. (The Museum of Modern Art/Film Stills Archive)

nation of sensitivity and authority that beautifully suits Lelouch's intimate style.

Semiimprovised acting plus Lelouch's visual style give the film a strange mixture of density and superficiality. On the one hand, the expressions, gestures, and inflections of the actors *are* the film, and they create an evolving relationship with notable subtlety. Trintignant's quiet enthusiasm meets Aimée's interested reserve, and a smile, a movement, or a brief physical contact can speak volumes. For once, two actors seem to be discovering love. Lelouch skillfully presents these gestures, which could easily become clichés, within convincing emotional climates. On the other hand, he neglects the conventional exposition and development that would give his characters more depth. For example, the main barrier inhibiting the relationship is Anne's powerful attachment to a dead man. This barrier remains relatively abstract (in contrast to the terrifying precision of a similar situation in *Hiroshima mon amour*) because we do not know that much about Anne and her loss. Lelouch evokes her pain, in flashback, rather than confronting it in the present. As Jean-Louis Comolli notes, Lelouch often cuts away from key dramatic moments.[9]

The scene where Jean-Louis, Anne, Françoise, and Antoine have Sunday brunch at a restaurant brings up another problem with Lelouch's approach. A long, large improvised scene, with several things going on at once, it captures the flux of relationships very well. The children bring the adults together, since they feel comfortable as parents on an outing. But the children also separate the adults by reacting with alarm when their parents start a private conversation. Despite this conflict, the scene is one of the few moments when Jean-Louis and Anne get to express themselves at length, and they are mutually charmed. The loose, informal style of the scene, marked by awkwardness from the adults and sudden outbursts from the children, undoubtedly adds to the scene's realistic and subtle effects. However, the hesitations of the actors also suggest a rather laborious improvisation. When Jean-Louis questions Anne about the movie business, we see not only Anne's reply but the surprised response of Anouk the actress. The play of levels is fascinating, but it can take the viewer out of the movie.[10] The spontaneity of the children is even more disturbing. They seem unmanipulated *except* by their "parents" (Trintignant and Aimée) who try to integrate their responses with the rest of the scene. So, spontaneity is modified by continuing intervention.

In many instances acting is dominated by visual style. For example, Lelouch presents several scenes of the main characters together in a car traveling between Paris and Deauville, usually at night. These scenes are mainly interesting as a visual metaphor, an extreme image of isolation. The characters exist in a self-enclosed world where external problems have been almost completely shut out.[11] Even the car radio, a possible link to the outside world, is only an annoyance. Lelouch achieves unusual intimacy by shooting closeups for these scenes from the hood of the car. The closeups are intercut by images of the car moving or the world seen through the window, so the car is both a living space and an image of motion, passion, and progress, pushing the characters toward a resolution. The self-contained car at night may also be an image of the mind's lucidity, broken by memories and dreams. Although the driving scenes do give the characters some chance to talk, the visual style carries most of the meaning.

Scenes of the characters at work form a kind of counterpoint to the love story. Instead of insisting monotonously on the main theme, Lelouch shows us the lyricism of work and of people who love their work. These scenes present the characters as competent, intelligent, and passionate people, and thus make their private uncertainties more touching. Further, the scenes of work suggest that there is an active, exciting world beyond the closed sphere of the love affair.

There is also a thematic relationship between the characters' professions and the love story. We have already discussed the car as a symbol of passion, progress, and activity. Lelouch creates a very nice opposition between the modern, active car and the timeless, passive ocean, a symbol both of Anne's emotionally "frozen" state and of immense possibility. The world of the cinema, where Anne works, is equally symbolic. It is a place where fantasies become concrete and dreams come true. This is most dramatically illustrated when a racing sequence is broken by a shock cut to four camels in a desert (part of a movie Anne is working on). The exotic tableau is also a surrealist image of awakening desire. More generally, the world of the movie set is the place where Anne met Pierre and fell in love. This may be a model for the whole of *A Man and a Woman*, which is a magic setting where two people fall in love.

A third function of the characters' professions is to provide spectacle and glamor for what might otherwise be a quiet, understated film. There is an element of escapism in showing so many racing and moviemaking scenes. Though these scenes do have a thematic meaning, they also glamorize the characters and move the film away from realism and toward sentimental romance. The beauty and excitement of many scenes tend to make the film a facile and agreeable spectacle independent of its other qualities. Lelouch has consistently objected to criticism of the film along these lines—for example, he told *Le Figaro Littéraire* that *A Man and a Woman* was not a "pretty," "easy" film but a serious study of Anne's psychological problem.[12] Still, it is clear that Lelouch's personal study of love is also an escapist romance.

A Man and a Woman represented France at the Cannes Film Festival in 1966 and shared the Grand Prize with Pietro Germi's *Signore e Signori*. *Signore e Signori* was soon forgotten, but Lelouch's film went on to an excellent commercial career in France and especially abroad. Whereas most French films play to a small, elite foreign audience, *A Man and a Woman* was a huge success all over the world. In the United States it played for extraordinary first runs of more than a year in several large cities (more than two years in Los Angeles) and eventually won Academy Awards for best screenplay and best foreign film. The film's success established Lelouch, after several years of obscurity, as a major French filmmaker.

One of the ironies of Lelouch's career is that he is still best known for this early film. *A Man and a Woman* was his biggest worldwide success, and it remains one of the two or three biggest international successes in the history of the French film industry. Another index of the film's popularity is the numerous uses which have been found for Lelouch's imagery (other films, television commercials) and especially Francis Lai's music (recordings from jazz to Muzak). All this for a simple, sentimental film without much depth! However, one can also look at the film in another way. Despite its flaws, *A Man and a Woman* is clever and inventive in many respects. Lelouch shows an astonishing ability to use technique and actors and metaphor and music to communicate a simple theme to the audience. The mass public demonstrated fairly good taste in responding to a film that is both stylistically original and emotionally engaging.

Live for Life (*Vivre pour vivre*, 1967)

For his next film, *Live for Life*, Lelouch took advantage of his new fame by using internationally known stars—Yves Montand, Annie Girardot, Candice Bergen—and some exotic locations. The film was shot in East Africa, Amsterdam, New York, and the French Alps as well as Paris. Lelouch had also planned to film on location in Vietnam (he shot some footage for the documentary *Far from Vietnam* while scouting locations for *Live for Life*), but the film's insurance company refused to allow this. Scenes set in Vietnam and the Congo were finally reconstructed in Camargue.[13]

In other respects, though, Lelouch remained faithful to the production methods of his low-budget films. *Live for Life* was shot by a very small crew in six weeks, with the director doing most of the camera work and improvising with the actors. Further, despite its ambitious subject matter and a few spectacular scenes, the film is basically an intimate study of three characters.

Robert Collomb (Yves Montand) is a successful television journalist whose private life is a series of adulteries and deceptions. Scenes of his work—newsreels from around the world, reporting trips to Africa and Vietnam—are intercut with his personal drama.

The film begins with Robert getting off a plane at Orly Airport and rushing to a hotel with his mistress. He checks out very quickly to return to Paris and to his wife, Catherine (Annie Girardot). But while leaving the hotel, he encounters Candice (Candice Bergen), a young American model who is checking into the hotel with her lover. Robert see Candice again at a boxing match—he is there with yet another woman—and talks his way into her hotel room later that night.

Candice goes with Robert on a reporting trip to Africa, where he interviews white mercenaries in the Congo. Then he takes Catherine to Amsterdam to celebrate the tenth anniversary of their meeting. Candice follows them and Robert invents an excuse to spend a day with her. Catherine discovers the ruse and leaves him. Six months later, Candice leaves Robert because he cannot forget Catherine.

Robert goes to Vietnam on an assignment and is missing for several days. Catherine, in Paris, and Candice, in New York, anxiously watch

Live for Life—Annie Girardot and Yves Montand. (United Artists)

Live for Life—Yves Montand and Candice Bergen. (United Artists)

the news for any word of him. However, neither contacts him on his return.

Robert seeks out Catherine at a ski resort and says he wants her back. She is very cool. They meet in a discotheque that evening, and again she shrugs him off. But when Robert returns to his car she is inside, waiting for him.

The plot of the film is pure soap opera—adventure, adultery, melodrama—but Lelouch's visual style makes *Live for Life* something more than a potboiler. The fever in which Robert lives is conveyed mainly by visual means. In an early scene, for example, we see him sitting glumly on a hotel bed while his mistress takes a shower in the background. Her image, nude behind a wall of frosted glass, suggests that Robert is obsessed by women but also removed from them. Later in this scene we see the couple in bed, with a zoom emphasizing the space between them. Clearly, Robert is not interested in the physical reality of adultery; something else is driving him.

The boxing match, a visual tour de force, is another important scene establishing the hero's attitude toward women. It begins with a flurry of blows shot in extreme close-up. The brown, glistening arms, half-seen in dim light, provide a highly charged erotic image as they flail at each other. At the bell, the crowd noise comes up and we cut to an intense, excited Robert sitting in the audience. After sending home mistress number two, Robert spots Candice in the crowd; close-ups show them exchanging glances in the darkened arena. The very rapid, sensual, and excited sporting event sets the tone not only for Robert's seduction of Candice but also for his desperation throughout the first part of the film. He is constantly trying to lose himself in new sensations.

Candice's arrival in Amsterdam is another visually stunning scene. A slow restaurant dinner between Robert and Catherine is intercut with Candice getting off a plane and coming into the city. The percussive theme accompanying these images suddenly gets much louder as Candice passes by the restaurant. Robert sees her, excuses himself, and they embrace in her hotel room. Then, in a brilliant shot, Lelouch pans from this embrace to the other side of the room, where he shows Robert and Candice arguing, and then back to their embrace. The pan is an ingenious way to show the distance between what Robert is doing and what he is thinking.

The film's strong visual style is further enhanced by a very interesting psychological and formal design. Robert, a communicator by profession, cannot communicate at all in his private life. His speech is a mass of banalities, lies, and half-truths; he is not able to talk sincerely about anything personal. However, this inability with language is compensated by a tremendous sensitivity to objects and sensations. Robert lives urgently and desperately in the mute world of the senses. By putting so much emphasis on vivid, sensuous, tactile images, Lelouch plunges us into Robert's subjective experience. Further, the fleeting, rapidly cut images suggest Robert's inability to control his world.

Lelouch counterpoints the preeminence of the visual with an occasional torrent of speech setting forth a character's innermost thoughts. Robert's monologue on the train from Amsterdam to Paris is especially important because for the first time he is able to tell the whole truth to Catherine. As the camera pans from one bunk to the other in their sleeping compartment, Robert slowly and painfully admits to his infidelity. The loud train noise here is perhaps an indication of just how difficult it is for Robert to talk. Catherine and Candice also express themselves in long monologues—Catherine speaking to the camera, Candice in an interior monologue from New York. Another related device is the song "Les Ronds dans l'eau," which comments, in French and English, on the love of the two women for Robert. The song is played over a montage of Catherine and Candice while Robert is in Vietnam.[14]

The three monologues and the song are a fascinating way to juxtapose the characters' internal impressions with an external view of them, but they are constructed a bit sloppily. Catherine's speech is marred by the absence of a defined context, and Candice's monologue is a pretentious musing on America and Vietnam. Even Robert's very moving confession is less than perfect because it seems for a while that we may be hearing an interior monologue rather than actual speech. Despite these problems, Lelouch deserves credit for using such bold formal devices.

Live for Life also attempts to go beyond the study of marriage and adultery. Lelouch, following the example of Alain Resnais and other modernist directors, uses Robert's story to explore the maze of interconnections between public life and private life, world events and the individual. *Life for Life* is clearly based on Resnais and Jorge Semprun's *La Guerre est finie* (1965). In that film Yves Montand plays an aging Spanish leftist who is torn between the pleasures of middle-class life in Paris and a continuing allegiance to a revolution that may never come. Lelouch has borrowed many things from this film: the tough and capable but disillusioned Montand character; the conflict between public and private personae; the anguish of a man caught in severe contradictions; even the attraction of two women, one young and one mature. *Live for Life* also slightly resembles Godard's *Pierrot le fou* (1965); in both films the Vietnam War casts a large shadow over the personal story.

Lelouch has added a good deal of his own to the interaction of personal and political. He makes the Montand character a newsman rather than a political activist, thus drawing on his own experience and con-

tinuing the study of media he began in *L'Amour avec des si*. The news
reports present world events in counterpoint to Robert's personal story.
Lelouch's hero is also much more integrated into society than those of
Resnais and Godard; his problem is a private malaise, rather than a total
crisis of conscience. A corollary to this distinction is that *Live for Life* is
to some extent a meditation on success, whereas *La Guerre est finie* and
Pierrot le fou are more concerned with failure and mortality.

Although he is less radical than Resnais or Godard, Lelouch does use
Live for Life as a forum for political commentary. His reconstructed
interview with white mercenaries in the Congo, supposedly based on
interviews with real mercenaries,[15] emphasizes their white-supremacist
and fascistic ideas. Robert's report on the Vietnam War calls it a tragedy
for the young men of both sides, but he adds that "America wants to
liberate Vietnam, but the bombing and napalm make this absurd."
Lelouch's Left-liberal orientation in this film was pointed out by French
journalists on both the Right and the Left.[16]

The use of the news reports to add a political dimension to the film is
certainly rich in possibilities; however, it also contains a major flaw.
Robert's personal problems are presented as a reaction to his work and
to world events. This is fine, except that the exact relationship between
Robert's psychology and the news is never spelled out. Does Robert feel
threatened by the violence and poverty surrounding his comfortable
European existence? Do the reports reflect part of his nature that he is
repressing? Is he troubled by the contradiction between his pose as an
authority figure and the actual instability of his life? Many other interpretations could be proposed.

Ambiguity is one of the more intriguing characteristics of the last
twenty years of filmmaking, but Lelouch can be faulted here for being
far too ambiguous. To describe a contradiction between public and
private life, on the model of *La Guerre est finie*, requires a very firm
notion of the relationship between them. Instead of developing this
relationship, Lelouch simply juxtaposes the news reports with Robert's
personal life. This ruins the film's grand design, and leaves the spectator
in limbo.

In other respects, *Live for Life* is a very uneven film. The constantly
moving camera, which is often extremely effective, can also be overly
indulgent. For example, the photo-safari scene in East Africa, featuring
a full-speed chase shot by three cameras, is exciting in itself but a quite
arbitrary way to make a point. Lelouch is trying to express the exhilaration of Robert and Candice's affair with a scene that seems extraneous to
the rest of the movie.[17] The film's music, very much in the vein of *A
Man and a Woman*, does not always fit *Live for Life*'s broader emotional
range. Among the actors, only Annie Giradot equals the performances
of *A Man and a Woman*. She combines the vulnerability of the Anouk

Aimée character with a much warmer and more adaptable nature. Yves Montand has a marvelously expressive face, but he seems stifled by the lack of action in the film. Young Candice Bergen, acting in a foreign language, is out of her depth. The other actors go unnoticed because of thoroughly undeveloped characters. For example, Catherine has a female friend who appears in several scenes, but to only one purpose: she shows that Catherine is not completely alone without Robert.

The final ski resort scenes of *Live for Life* are particularly uneven. Their easy symbolism—snow as purity, a discotheque as modern decadence—oversimplifies the film's political-personal theme. Catherine is accompanied by a variety of young friends whom the filmmaker never really introduces. The sound in the discotheque scene is poorly handled, with a recorded rock song not matching the musicians on stage, and Francis Lai's theme music breaking in weirdly from time to time (in general, the sound in *Live for Life* does not have the sophistication one would expect from a film of this quality). On the other hand, Lelouch has put together a nice montage of Robert, isolated and withdrawn, at the dinner table with Catherine's animated friends, and by using a discotheque named the "Zoom" he tells a joke on himself. The film ends with a beautiful image that exemplifies the virtues of Lelouch's informal, hand-held camera style. The camera catches Robert in a medium close-up with a slight upward angle at the moment he notices Catherine in the car. The imperfect, candid quality of the hand-held, asymmetrical, and very dark shot creates a complicity between Robert and the spectator. Robert starts to make a movement, then the image freezes. By ending in half-darkness, in the middle of a movement, and before Robert commits himself, Lelouch has created an extraordinary image of uncertainty.

The strong point of *A Man and a Woman* was that form and content fit together so well that any awkwardness seemed inconsequential. Although it is in some ways a more accomplished film, *Live for Life* does not have the same unity and coherence. The political theme never really fits into the personal story, and so the film becomes an assemblage of pieces, some brilliant and others not very good. *Live for Life* is an interesting mixture of melodrama, psychology, politics, and spectacle that does not quite realize its ambitions.

Life, Love, Death (*La Vie, l'amour, la mort*, 1968)

The starting point of *Life, Love, Death* was a book called *Tu ne tueras pas* [*Thou Shalt Not Kill*] by Albert Naud, a prominent French attorney.[18] The book, a vivid and sensationalized work of nonfiction, is described by its author as an attack on the public's tolerance of capital punishment.[19] The book includes a long, extremely detailed account of a condemned man's last hours, a discussion of the role of chance in trials and murders, and even a gruesome description of how decapitated heads die very slowly. When Lelouch decided to make a film about capital punishment, he engaged Naud as a consultant. Later, Naud was convinced to play the role of the defense attorney in the film.

Life, Love, Death was originally planned as a one-hour television show. Lelouch was going to reconstruct, in meticulous detail, the most impressive part of Naud's book—the description of the last hour of a condemned man. The television film was to be made very quickly, because Lelouch had more ambitious projects in mind: *Toute la vie d'un homme*, which years later became *Toute une vie; Le dernier des juifs*, about what would happen if Hitler had won the war; and *Le Big Boss*, about gambling.[20] However, Lelouch became interested in the biography and psychology of his condemned man, and so he expanded the one-hour reconstruction into a fictional feature film.

The story concerns François Toledo (Amidou), a North African immigrant who works at the Simca factory and lives in a small apartment with his wife (Janine Magnan) and child. Toledo also spends a few hours a week with his blond mistress Caroline (Caroline Cellier), whom he met at the Simca plant. This Everyman figure is arrested, interrogated, tried, convicted, and sentenced to death for the strangulation of three prostitutes. The film concludes with the process of preparing Toledo for death, ending as the guillotine blade is coming down.

Most of the film's interest comes from the way Lelouch tells the story. Description of the crime is withheld until the last possible moment, so, for much of the film, Toledo seems to be a simple man hounded by the police. His outing to the country with Caroline becomes a kind of persecution fantasy as police stand by with loaded guns at the doors of their motel room. In a later scene, the police break into a hotel room to arrest Toledo and Caroline without explanation; their only crime seems to be adultery.

Lelouch withholds crucial information through the interrogation and the trial. Much of the interrogation is without dialogue (only music), although a few suggestive lines about prostitutes, murder, and the death penalty are thrown in. The trial is shown with musical accompaniment until the sentencing, which is spoken. Unfortunately, the suppression of so much dialogue comes off as extremely manipulative, since Lelouch is obviously hiding something. The elliptical montages may be following the mental state of Toledo, who does not appear to be fully aware of what is happening. However, the montages are too loose and disjointed to be a convincing subjective vision.

The prison scenes are more successful. They begin with a tremendous

Life, Love, Death—Caroline Cellier *(left)* and Amidou *(extreme right).* At the police station. (Lopert Pictures)

shock: as Toledo leaves the courtroom the film switches from color to black-and-white to indicate the end of his liberty and hope. This is the most stunning use of color variation in all of Lelouch's films. In the scenes that follow, mise-en-scène as well as color show the loss of hope. Instead of the frenetic movement of Lelouch's usual style, we see fixed, close-up images (Toledo's face, his shoe, a newspaper headline about a long weekend) emphasizing the immobility and despair of the situation. One memorable image from the top of the cell shows the room distorting (because of a wide-angle lens), suggesting the psychological pressure of confinement.

Toledo's crimes are finally revealed in flashbacks, accompanied by voice-overs from the trial. The flashbacks are naturally in color, since they refer to a time before the death sentence. The first flashback image is, in fact, a traditional image of innocence and freedom—a *bal de campagne*. However, the flashbacks do show that Toledo is guilty of strangling three women because he was humiliated by being impotent with them. The flashback narrative leads inevitably back to the courtroom and to the sentencing.

After another scene of the death sentence, the images switch from color to sepia, perhaps indicating the netherworld situation of waiting for death. The guillotine is built, and Toledo is blessed and prepared for slaughter. The image freezes as spectators watch the blade coming down and a voice-over preaches: "If you ever saw an execution, you would never vote for the death penalty again."

The effect of this complicated structure is to involve the spectator with Toledo's point of view. At the beginning of the film we see Toledo's bewilderment and pain as he loses his freedom and goes through arrest, trial, and imprisonment. By the time we discover the crimes he has committed, we do not reject him. He is certainly not a monster; he is, instead, depressed and sick. So, we continue to empathize with Toledo, dedspite our awareness of his guilt, through his imprisonment and execution. Lelouch's manipulation of the spectator generally works, although some scenes too clearly announce themselves as manipulative.

The film is an extraordinary exercise in subjectivity. Plot, locations, and acting are realistic,[21] but this provides only a convincing backdrop for Lelouch's evocation of how it feels to be condemned to death. The film's unique narrative structure makes us identify with Toledo, and visual style fills in the connotations of his world. Rapid, fragmented editing shows Toledo's disorientation and confusion. The dominant visual motif is enclosure, both before and after his imprisonment. Even when Toledo spends time with his girl friend, the police are following him, trapping him. The many scenes of prison routine show how helpless and insignificant Toledo is in the judicial system. Dark shadows and sepia tones in the final scenes help end the film on a note of desperation and terror. Lelouch's ability to plunge us into the experience of the condemned man is the film's great strength.

Amidou's performance as François Toledo could also be considered subjective, because the actor submerges himself in the character's personality. Amidou was chosen at least partly because, as an actor unknown to film audiences, he could be very closely identified with the character he played. He was "trained" for his role for a period of months: he dressed like Toledo, worked in the Simca plant, attended trials, and spent time in prison. During the course of filming, Amidou was never shown a script and never allowed to revert to his normal personality. He was interrogated for eight hours, imprisoned, and dragged off to the guillotine.[22] The result, at least in this particular film, is impressive. We see an average man, perhaps a bit troubled, who literally comes apart as he is subjected to the judicial process. Most of this is done simply through shots of Amidou's face, although his soft, defeated voice adds to the overall impression. Just before death Amidou-Toledo completely loses control, and his anguished attempt to avoid the inevitable is difficult to watch.

Before shooting *Life, Love, Death*, Lelouch described the film like this: "What it's about for me is to create in the spectator a certain number of emotions, and not to argue against the death penalty."[23] The

Life, Love, Death—Amidou. On the way to the guillotine. (Lopert Pictures)

film certainly succeeds on this level. However, it is also an argument against capital punishment, and that argument is not always strong. The narrative itself suggests that Toledo should be spared, but it is too convoluted to be a simple, clear statement against capital punishment. The general implications of Toledo's case are discussed mainly in voice-overs (by Lelouch, the defense attorney, and the prosecutor). These speeches, formally separated from the story, do not always mesh with the emotional flow of images. For example, a voice-over by the defense attorney describes how chance is an important character in every trial. This is one of the most sophisticated points in Naud's book, proposing that the death penalty is unfair because trials and sentences are so heavily influenced by the psychology of the people involved.[24] In Lelouch's film the subtlety of the point is lost, and the passage becomes a confusing suggestion that perhaps Toledo is innocent after all.

Another problem with the film's argument is the question of responsibility. Courtroom dramas are often used to criticize an idea, a society, a concept of human nature, but Lelouch does not have an indictment of society in mind. The judge, the lawyers, and the prison system are all viewed positively. Even the police, who seem brutal and arbitrary at first, are justified by later developments. The film puts all the blame for capital punishment on the laws themselves. It does not deal with why those laws are there, and thus leaves an important area unresolved.

Despite its limits, *Life, Love, Death* marks an important step forward for Lelouch. He moves away from the glamor and success of *A Man and a Woman* and *Live for Life* to make a "difficult" film on a controversial topic. *Life, Love, Death* shows that Lelouch's style can work for a wide variety of subjects; in fact, it is probably his most successful experiment with subjectivity. The film also demonstrates Lelouch's desire to be something more than a box office success.

Un Homme qui me plaît (Love Is a Funny Thing, 1969)

Un Homme qui me plaît takes place mainly in the United States, where Françoise (Annie Girardot), an actress, and Henri (Jean-Paul Belmondo), a composer, are working on the same Hollywood film. Brought together by their Frenchness, the two sleep together one night even though both are married. Then, on an impulse, they take a short vacation in the American Southwest: Las Vegas, Lake Powell, a restored Western town, Monument Valley, and finally New Orleans. Before leaving for Europe they promise to break up their marriages and to meet in a few days in Nice. Françoise shows up at the Nice airport; Henri does not.

The movie that Françoise and Henri are making is not a major emphasis of the film, but rather a means of commenting on the love story. No one takes the film-within-a-film very seriously. Henri comments to its director that there is not one interesting character in his movie: the people are rich, famous, they travel on a whim; who cares about such things today? The director replies that Henri's music will disguise the flaws. This exchange points directly at *Un Homme qui me plaît*, in which Lelouch's objective is to make us care about rich, leisured people living out a small love story. In a later scene Henri talks about writing false music for false Westerns. Still, the film seems to be saying, the result is somehow true.

The travelogue through the United States is not tremendously exciting, either. Tourism is shown as banal, commercialized, and only mildly amusing. The film's tourist's-eye view of the United States does have an interesting strangeness. We see a garish motel room in Las Vegas, complete with slot machine; an impassive Navaho selling tires; a discussion of French money in a roadside café. But Lelouch presents these observations in a very loose, undramatic way; they are simply sights along the road.

Un Homme qui me plaît seems to be about a casual, unimportant love affair in a banal setting. Lelouch describes the film as "the story of a love affair that lasts the time of a parenthesis, the time of a voyage, the time of a film production."[25] However, the film also has a hidden theme: the possibility that the affair will develop into a more serious relationship. Most of the film is concerned with whether the love affair is a casual, carefree adventure or a real and important meeting between two people. Lelouch says (continuing the statement just quoted), "This film is in the image of a doubt, because nothing will ever be given as definitive. The love that will unite Jean-Paul Belmondo and Annie Girardot is a perpetual contestation of the couple. . . ."[26]

Thus, the film becomes another Lelouch experiment with connotation. The fragile, contingent relationship between Françoise and Henri is viewed only obliquely, through the tourism and casual banter. Their romance has no big scenes, no serious talks, no action, no plot. Instead, Lelouch hints at hidden depths through the comportment of the actors and the nuances of the mise-en-scène. He works subtlety into a story that is intentionally light and almost trivial.

Making a film about banality is very dangerous, because one risks boring the spectator. Lelouch does not totally avoid this danger. Many of his dynamic images are undercut by a sense that they are only superficial, only tourism. They have a certain appeal as spectacle, but do not connect with the film's deeper concerns. Much of the film limps along from one mildly amusing scene to the next. A few moments do capture the excitement of a new affair: a splash in a pool, the complicity of being caught in bed together by a hotel employee. One memorable fantasy scene shows the couple's car attacked by Indians as Henri describes the orchestration of music for Westerns. This is a fine illustration of the powers of a persuasive, imaginative talker.

The best thing about *Un Homme qui me plaît* is the performance of Annie Girardot as Françoise. Her character is a mature, sensitive woman, not so detached and liberated as she originally appears. She has a quick wit, but her eyes show an essential seriousness and vulnerability. Even her lightest remarks are honest and sincere. For example, when Henri asks. "Do you do this often?", she replies, "Whenever I meet a man who pleases me ["un homme qui me plaît"]—which is very rare." Françoise does not easily commit herself; she protects herself with irony, but her solid, serious personality gives the story a sense of possibility that it might not otherwise have had.

Françoise's two most important scenes take place in Europe. In the first, a tremendously intimate, understated scene, she tells her husband (Marcel Bozzuffi) that she no longer loves him. The mutual respect, caring, and understanding between characters here contrasts vividly with the studied casualness of the American idyll. This scene also shows that the vacation adventure will affect other people's lives. Even better is the scene at the airport. Close-ups of Françoise at the gate alternate with shots of the plane landing and passengers getting off. A slightly sad Francis Lai theme plays over the images, but the theme could easily

Un Homme qui me plaît—Jean-Paul Belmondo and Annie Girardot. (Academy of Motion Picture Arts and Sciences)

modulate to a major key with Henri's appearance. Françoise stands bravely and sturdily as the plane empties, the music gets louder, and Henri never appears. Many emotions play across her face—joy, sadness, anger, calm, confusion, ironic understanding. When the plane is empty, Françoise laughs sadly, she moves her lips, and she looks down. This close-up lasts fifteen seconds, and the film ends. The entire scene is a superb performance by Girardot, communicating expectation and disappointment without words and with barely a gesture.

The Belmondo character is quite different. Though he is boyishly good-looking and athletic, an accomplished liar and a carefree spirit, he lacks the great charm one would expect of a Don Juan figure. He often treats Françoise more as a buddy than as a woman. Belmondo plays the role in a loose and casual way, often mugging for the camera. It is difficult to criticize his performance, because he is supposed to be shallow. The difference in performance (Girardot: a hidden depth; Belmondo: all surface) goes directly to the film's theme. Still, a more appealing seducer might have increased our empathy for Françoise.

Un Homme qui me plaît is certainly an odd film, a film that presents itself as superficial. Lelouch does manage to describe, in a low-key way, the problems of a woman caught between a casual modern life-style and more traditional psychological needs. Other than that, the film is a kind of sketchbook of moviemaking, tourism, and the United States.

Conclusions

The films from *A Man and a Woman* to *Un Homme qui me plaît* present a thoroughly subjective vision. In each film, Lelouch is mainly interested in the feelings of two or three characters. He creates a turbulent flow of emotions corresponding to their situations. Realism bends to express emotion, as in the formal experiments of *Live for Life* (the monologues, the imagined argument) or the evocation of waiting for death in *Life, Love, Death*. Each film also has a strong connotative tone. *A Man and a Woman* is sentimental; *Live for Life* is jaded; *Life, Love, Death* is desperate; *Un Homme qui me plaît* is banal. Jean Collet describes Lelouch's filmmaking at the time of *Life, Love, Death* as "primitive," "naive," and "visceral,"[27] because of the force of his emotions. Lelouch is certainly a romantic in this period.

The roots of Lelouch's subjectivity in these films lie in an ambivalence shared by the director and his characters. On the one hand, the films of the late 1960s shows the private difficulties of lonely, vulnerable people. Anne is still tied to her dead husband; Robert's life is a mass of lies; Toledo has a schizoid attraction-repulsion to prostitutes; Françoise and Henri almost find an important relationship. All of these characters are overwhelmed by their emotions, and yet they have great difficulty relating to other people. Even the simplest things, such as talking honestly to a wife or lover, become problematic. Lelouch at times connects these difficulties to the rapid changes and dislocations of modern life, but he never loses sight of the personal.

On the other hand, the films have a much more pleasant aspect. The characters are attractive, successful people who appear to live comfortably in a pleasant and glamorous environment. François Toledo is less comfortable than the others, but even he enjoys a weekend trip to the country. Many scenes in the films are light, lively, sometimes humorous. Lelouch's moving camera often expresses exuberance, a zest for living. And the characters do make a few hesitant steps toward solving their problems. Françoise tries to make something of a chance love affair, and Caroline seems to have cured Toledo. Love is difficult but still possible in these films.

The impression that emerges from the clash of viewpoints is a very basic confusion. Life is desperate; it is also pleasant, amusing, and joyous. Moods change from anguish to exhilaration in a moment. One vaguely senses the falseness and superficiality of modern life, but political thinking is swamped by a more general disorientation. The characters are thrown back on their own subjectivity becaue experience is so disorganized.

Lelouch's stylistic innovations all express this kind of confusion. His fragmented and extremely varied images suggest a constantly changing world dominated by emotion. In *Live for Life* and *Life, Love, Death* the fragmentation specifically shows that Robert and Toledo are out of control, driven by unconscious needs. Francis Lai's insistent music, in all the films but especially *A Man and a Woman* and *Live for Life*, again suggests the power of feelings. The characters do not decide or discuss or agree; they feel. Music often expresses this imperative, as in the scene in which Anne, making love with Jean-Louis, obsessively recalls Pierre. Lelouch's approach to acting also stresses the subjective. His characters feel (respond, react, show emotion) more than they act (work, do something, accomplish a purpose).

The subjective style does have certain drawbacks. It works best on simple, intimate stories, since it dispenses with exposition and objectivity. Anything beyond the sphere of the couple is seen through the protagonists' limited vision. Lelouch's semi-improvised shooting method also has its problems. The freshness and subtlety of his direction are balanced by inconsistency and a lack of depth. The actors, although generally effective, are sometimes constrained by their passive roles. Beyond these problems of style lies a more fundamental question. The theme of confusion is a valid response to a confused period, where affluence mixes with uncertainty and anxiety. The same theme can be found in films by Godard, Fellini, Antonioni, and Bergman. But what comes after confusion? Lelouch suggests only that love may tentatively resolve the characters' personal dramas. He repeats a subjective and sentimental treatment four times and thus lessens the impact of a provocative starting point.

In *A Man and a Woman* it is very attractive to see the world presented in basic and even solvable terms. The film is about private life; everything else is seen as inessential. Love is difficult but possible. The originality of Lelouch's style masks the thinness of his concept. He cleverly, if unevenly, extends his study of private life to a broader social context in *Live for Life* and *Life, Love, Death*. With *Un Homme qui me plaît*, though, the limitations of subject and style have already become familiar and obvious.

3
Collective Projects

In the late 1960s, after making *A Man and a Woman*, Lelouch was involved in a number of ambitious projects in addition to making his own feature films. He participated in the collective antiwar film *Far from Vietnam;* he made a documentary about the Winter Olympics with François Reichenbach and six other cameramen; he produced several feature films by young directors; and he was involved in the May 1968 debate over reorganizing the French cinema. We can only speculate on the reasons for Lelouch's involvement in these projects. Perhaps, as an outsider in the French film industry, he threw himself into collective activities when he got the chance. Perhaps he felt guilty about his sudden wealth—thus, the project for helping other directors. Perhaps his moderate-Left politics, expressed in *Live for Life* and *Life, Love, Death*, led logically to these collective projects.

Far from Vietnam (Lion de Vietnam, 1967) is a political protest film made by a large and prominent group of French filmmakers: directors Alain Resnais, William Klein, Joris Ivens, Agnès Varda, Claude Lelouch, and Jean-Luc Godard; news reporter Michèle Ray; writer Jacques Sternberg; composer Michel Fano; actor Bernard Fresson; and many more artists and technicians. The film was organized and edited by Chris Marker, Jacqueline Meppiel, and Andréa Haran. It includes documentary sequences from France, the United States, and Vietnam, plus fictional sketches by Resnais and Godard. The subject is first, an analysis of the Vietnam War, and second, a discussion of how the war relates to the filmmakers. One notable aspect of this project is the broad range of political opinion represented, from the moderate Lelouch to the Communist Ivens and the radical-Left Marker.

Lelouch's image of U.S. aircraft carriers in the Gulf of Tonkin open and close the film. The first sequence begins at dawn, as bombs are hoisted from long, narrow supply barges to the huge carriers. Strange, dawn colors (blue ships, bombs, and water; red sky and ships' lights) highlight the unnaturalness of a machine-dominated world. Lelouch's swooping, panning camera follows the bombs as they swing freely on a line from barge to carrier; the motion in all directions suggests an out-of-control technology. A narrator announces: "On one side, the United States of America. Each morning the carriers in the Gulf of Tonkin get their supply of bombs, one thousand tons a day."

The film then cuts to a sequence by Joris Ivens: a still image of a field, with the dominant colors yellow and white. Camouflaged North Vietnamese soldiers rise out of the field, move a few paces, and sink back into the vegetation. The narrator states: "On the other side, the people of Vietnam."

After the film's lengthy credits, we return to the aircraft carriers. Crews load bombs onto the planes, each brief shot ending in an upward movement. Then we see a montage of takeoffs, Lelouch following each plane on its upward curve. The power and excitement of the planes are tempered by our realization of their destructiveness: they will undoubtedly be used against the Vietnamese presented by Ivens, the soldier-peasants in the field or perhaps the civilians building bomb shelters in his next sequence.

The film's opening section thus beautifully defines the two sides in Vietnam: the rich Americans with their huge machines of destruction and the poor, human-scale, close-to-nature Vietnamese. Both directors present textbook examples of how film can communicate through composition, movement, color, and editing. Although the visual portraits are certainly simplified, they provide a concise and provocative introduction to the film.

Lelouch's shots of the carriers being loaded are repeated at the end of the film. This repetition underscores a dilemma which is considered at great length in *Far from Vietnam:* despite protests (including the film), the destructive Vietnam War goes on. Lelouch's carriers and bombs are a metonymic image of the continuing war.

In 1967 and 1968, Lelouch thought enough of *Far from Vietnam* to distribute it through Les Films 13. However, he now says that the film is "dishonest,"[1] and that he "detests" this film because filmmakers who disagree should not make a political film together.[2] Lelouch, as one of the most moderate contributors to the film, may very well object to something in it. He did not do the editing,[3] and he may object, for example, to the juxtaposition of his images with Ivens's heroic picture of the North Vietnamese. Although Lelouch's sequences of *Far from Vietnam* are an important part of the film, he now disowns his participation in the project.

Lelouch had much more control over *Grenoble (13 Jours en France),* a feature-length documentary about the Winter Olympics of 1968. He co-directed the film with François Reichenbach, an old friend whose impressionistic, intimate, hand-held camera style of documentary filmmaking seems to be the approximate equivalent of Lelouch's approach to fiction. The actual filming was done by eight cameramen: Lelouch, Reichenbach, Jean-Pierre and Jean-Paul Janssen, Willy Bogner, Jean Collomb, Guy Gilles, and Pierre Willemin. Lelouch then edited the many hours of footage into a two-hour movie (the American version is shorter), and released it through Les Films 13.

Lelouch and Reichenbach describe the film as an attempt to capture the details, anecdotes, and emotions surrounding the Olympics.[4] The athletic events are shown, but not stressed. The film has no dialogue or commentary, so the suspense of competition is generally lost. Often the filmmakers do not even identify the athletes: the spectator is supposed to recognize Jean-Claude Killy, Peggy Fleming, the Goitschell sisters, and the other stars of this Olympics. The film does show the beauty and the effort of sport, but it treats the crowds, bands, police, nightlife, and other sights of the games as equally important.

The filmmakers had at one time planned to integrate the documentary footage of the Olympics with a fictional love story about a foreign journalist and a French girl.[5] They eventually dropped this idea, says Lelouch, because the documentary material was so strong.[6] Looking at the finished film, one wonders about their decision. The film does have a general point of view—it sees the Olympics as a huge, hectic carnival in the snow—but lacks organization and coherence. Many individual images and scenes are excellent—the camera-on-skis work by Willy Bogner, the high-spirited nightlife scenes in sepia, the superb ski-jump montage. However, Lelouch (as editor) seems to have only a very loose idea of showing the variety and emotion of the festival. He has trouble with transitions, with crowd scenes, and with picturesque images that do not fit together. The resulting film is energetic but ragged.

The same criticism cannot be made of Francis Lai and Pierre Barouh's musical score. The music consists of four basic songs: a lyrical theme song, an exciting action theme, a song to Jean-Claude Killy, and a song to Peggy Fleming. These songs, sometimes orchestral, sometimes with words, are alternated with live sound and a few passages of silence. Barouh's lyrics add a pointed commentary on the games. His most notable effort is an ironic ode to Killy, stressing the fleeting and derisory character of fame. The sound track is extremely well organized and provides the film with a fine lyrical framework. It gives us a taste of what *Grenoble* could have been.

Although Lelouch's dynamic style should be well suited to at least some kinds of documentary filmmaking, his major documentaries—*La Femme Spectacle, Pour un maillot jaune,* and *Grenoble*—all suffer from being too diffuse. His imagination seems to need the discipline of working from a narrative. In *Grenoble,* he has the further handicap of working with eight cameramen instead of doing all the photography himself.

Grenoble opening in Paris just after the political upheaval of May

1968 and was criticized for not reflecting the turmoil and contestation of that period. The film is not apolitical: Barouh's lyrics on Peggy Fleming ("J'ai honte pour Peggy") are strongly anti-American and anti-Vietnam War, and a grim hockey match between Russia and Czechoslovakia points up the tension between those two nations. Newspaper headlines about Vietnam show that world crises continue during the Olympic games. The film also mildly pokes fun at General de Gaulle's autocratic manner in the grandstand. However, *Grenoble* does present an untroubled, traditional, festive view of France that was out of fashion by the time the film was released. This, plus the problem of coherence, may explain the film's poor commercial showing.

In 1967, Lelouch announced another ambitious collective project. He would produce a number of low-budget films, some by established directors like Godard, Reichenbach, and Peter Watkins, and others by newcomers. Financing and distribution for these films plus any Lelouch would direct would be provided by United Artists, Les Films Ariane (Alexandre Mnouchkine and Georges Dancigers), and Les Films 13. At least some of the films that were to be made would be chosen on the basis of first a screenplay and then filming a ten-minute "essay" to show the quality of the director and his script. French television also participated, at least briefly, in the scheme of co-producing and exhibiting the first film essays. Lelouch and his partners thus attempted, in a modest way, to reform the French production system.

The agreement with United Artists and Films Ariane covered only ten total films, but when the agreement came to an end, Lelouch continued to produce films by other directors. Among the films he coproduced in the late 1960s and early 1970s are *Les Gauloises bleues* (1967), by critic Michel Cournot; *Une Infinie Tendresse* (1968), by Pierre Jallaud; *Clair de Terre* (1969), by Guy Gilles; *L'Américain* (1969), by Marcel Bozzuffi; *Camarades* (1969), by Marin Karmitz; *Le Maître du temps* (1969), by Jean-Daniel Pollet; *Ça n'arrive qu'aux autres* (1970), by Nadine Trintignant; *Comme dans la vie* (1972), by Pierre Willemin; and *Le Far-West* (1972), by Jacques Brel. Lelouch also financed a major reediting of the classic *Napoléon* (1927) by its author, Abel Gance. The only common denominator between these films is that they are all "difficult," noncommercial works; otherwise, they reflect Lelouch's broad tastes as a filmgoer. The disturbed adolescent of *Les Gauloises bleues* and the handicapped children of *Une Infinie Tendresse* and *Ça n'arrive qu'aux autres* may be extreme versions of Lelouch's isolated, vulnerable adults, but *Camarades* is a Leftist political film and *Le Maître du temps* is science fiction.

Lelouch was also involved in the French film industry's activities during May 1968. With Louis Malle, Truffaut, and Godard, Lelouch was instrumental in closing down the Cannes Film Festival of 1968, even though *Les Gauloises bleues* and *Grenoble* were scheduled to play at the festival. He then participated in the Etats-Généraux du Cinéma, a conference called to restructure the French film industry. Part of the agenda at the conference was a system to aid young directors, analogous to what Lelouch was already doing privately. However, Lelouch did not respond positively to the events of May 1968. He has disparaged this period of social protest in several films; for example, in *And Now My Love* the hero's response to a demonstration is "I prefer to work alone. So, no politics." Lelouch has remained very active in the French film world in the 1970s, but he has avoided collective projects.

4
The Crime File

The Crook (Le Voyou, 1970)

The Crook (Le Voyou, 1970) is a very complicated film full of flashbacks
and other narrative tricks. The barest outline of the plot (ignoring tricks)
goes like this: Simon the Swiss (Jean-Louis Trintignant) carries out an
incredibly clever kidnapping of a young boy, assisted by his girl friend
Martine (Christine Lelouch) and by Charlot (Charles Gérard). The boy's
father (Charles Denner) is not rich but he works for a bank, and Simon
correctly figures that the bank will pay a large ransom for the boy rather
than face unfavorable publicity. However, Simon is double-crossed by
Denner, a hidden accomplice, and goes to jail. Five years later Simon
breaks out of jail, arranges his affairs, and, after a series of adventures,
takes a plane for New York with Charlot. Unfortunately, bad weather
diverts the plane to Montreal, where the police may be waiting. . . .

The Crook marks an important break in Lelouch's career. His previous films feature passive characters caught up in their emotions. These
characters do not control their lives; they simply experience them. Simon, on the other hand, is an active character who dominates his emotions and his environment. Similarly, where the previous films are
intimate, sentimental, and melodramatic, *The Crook* is a distanced,
comic adventure film. The contrast even extends to production methods
and music: the films of the late 1960s have a great deal of improvisation
to express emotion, whereas *The Crook* is a more structured, less improvised movie; *A Man and a Woman* and *Live for Life* have elaborate,
sentimental scores, whereas *The Crook* relies on variations of one brash
theme.

Psychologically, Simon the Swiss resembles many of the characters of
the earlier films. He is an isolated, withdrawn person who has trouble
relating to others. A shot of Simon in his cell, bathed in strong white
light, presents him as the perfect image of alienated man. However,
instead of simply accepting his fate, Simon chooses a life of adventure
and risk. He tries to dominate whatever situation he is in, using wit,

The Crook—Jean-Louis Trintignant. (United Artists)

force, planning, and deceit. Even his shyness becomes an asset, giving him a shield to eliminate inessentials and a critical distance to facilitate planning. Simon's choice of adventure also gives the film a comic edge, since one aspect of the active life is a sense that everything is malleable, and therefore not to be taken too seriously.

A key to understanding Simon is the environment in which he works. The Paris of *The Crook* is clean, rich, new, abstract, and empty. It has been taken over by publicity and by a Madison Avenue-style modernism. Shiny surfaces, luxurious decors, and high technology cannot hide the mediocrity of this world. The "average Frenchmen" of the film are weak, nervous, and corrupt. For example, despite the machinations of the Charles Denner character, he and his wife (played by Judith Magre) are essentially hapless victims of a society they don't understand. The small-time hoods with whom Simon deals are equally weak and corrupt, despite the appearances of a beyond-the-law camaraderie. Deception is a way of life; Simon is betrayed to the police three times in the course of the film, and survives only by consistently deceiving in his turn. In these circumstances, the independent gangster's skill and daring are attractive and even liberating.

The film's narrative structure echoes both Simon's bravura and the theme of deception. Lelouch's technique is as exuberant as ever, but here he ties it to an intricate narrative pattern. Virtuoso moments suggest the hero's brilliance, while the complexity of the narrative evokes a world that is complicated but still, to some extent, controllable. Many scenes surprise the viewer. The camera may start on an isolated detail, and then move back to establish the scene. Lelouch also plays with flashbacks and deceptive plot twists. His most amazing trick involves a hidden flashback. A discussion of a hideout seems to lead logically to a scene at that hideout, but actually the film moves back five years at this point. The spectator eventually discovers that there has been a time jump, but it takes more than one viewing to figure out when the jump occurred. The unusual flashback is part of the process by which the spectator discovers the film through a web of deceptions.

The credit sequence, another virtuoso moment, features a "gangster ballet" of machine guns, old cars, and pretty girls. In the foreground, dancer Victor Upshaw sings (in English) the film's theme song, which describes both the glory of the gangster hero and his inevitable fall. This lovely sequence, an homage to both the American gangster film and the American musical comedy, turns out to be a film-within-a-film that Simon is watching. So, instead of setting up the plot, the sequence comments metaphorically on what we will see—deceptions, gangsters, excitement, comedy mixed with seriousness. The "gangster ballet" incidentally shows that Lelouch could be a fine director of musical comedies.

The kidnapping is Lelouch's, and Simon's, most sustained invention. It begins as Martine, gleefully simulating a radio announcer, calls Denner's family to announce they have won a new Simca car. Martine has no trouble bringing the family into her game, even making them shout "Merci, Simca" into the telephone. Father, mother, and son, following Martine's instructions, rush to the Olympia Music Hall for a show featuring singer Sacha Distel. They leave their son Daniel outside with Simon, supposedly the Simca publicist. Thus, the victim is literally handed to his kidnappers.

The scene is a clever satire on publicity. Clearly, the kidnapper-publicists can get anything they want from the average French family. They offer material wealth, the recognition of being on the radio, and the excitement of the Distel show. Denner and Magre are delighted to make fools of themselves for Simca—and a look at any audience-participation television show will confirm how accurate Lelouch's satire is. He demonstrates both the great power of publicity and the ease with which it can be manipulated for all sorts of ends. Perhaps the publicists are the real criminals.

Simon's battle of nerves with the bank is even more revealing of social corruption and the power of publicity. Simon and the director of the

The Crook—Jean-Louis Trintignant and Christine Lelouch. Simon visits with his ex-wife. (United Artists)

bank (Jacques Doniol-Valcroze) give identical speeches on why the bank must pay to avoid a public outcry and loss of business. Publically, however, the bank acts only for the highest motives; Gérard Sire, once again the radio announcer, gives an ironic speech praising the bank's "élan humanitaire." In a further twist, the forced ransom becomes good publicity for the bank, resulting in a large number of new customers. As Doniol-Valcroze announces with immense satisfaction, "Our generous gesture has become a paying gesture." Then, in another cynical move for publicity, he gives Denner an important promotion.

In this basically corrupt world, Lelouch discovers a value that was lacking in the sentimental films—friendship. Friendship seems to be a corollary of action, a bond created by working together.[1] Simon says he always works alone, stressing his independence, but he has three friends in the film. Martine is both Simon's girl friend and his daring accomplice during the kidnapping. Later, though, she marries an industrialist, the "Yogurt King" of France, and betrays Simon. Danièle Delorme plays a timid secretary who helps Simon after his escape, first involuntarily and then willingly. She is attracted not only by Simon but by the excitement of his outlaw status. The most important friend is Charlot, a loyal, longtime accomplice who is the one person Simon can trust. Charlot's presence makes *The Crook* much warmer and more comic; instead of one isolated crook we have two friends laughing at the world. The role is beautifully played by the simple, blunt, and extremely droll Charles Gérard. Gérard, a film director himself, was not an actor before *The Crook;* Lelouch chose him because "He is like that in real life."[2] He has become a kind of icon of friendship in Lelouch's later films.

Like the other "movie brats" of his generation (especially Godard and Truffaut), Lelouch is very sensitive to the metaphoric implications of film genres. He specifically presents Simon as a movie gangster. The film's title and credit sequence connect this "voyou" to all the outlaw heroes of the past. Methods change, but the gangster's toughness and independence remain. However, Lelouch also updates his hero in relation to the contemporary world. Simon can be seen as the last individualist. He is not a violent, desperate rebel, but an attractive, talented person who decided that crime offered more opportunity than legitimate business. Lelouch, in an interview, points out the character's intelligence, saying that he has the ability to be a political boss, an artist, or president of France.[3] In the superficial, empty Paris of the film, Simon is probably right to turn to crime. Compare, for example, Simon with Martine's husband, the Yogurt King. The Yogurt King is a successful and decent man, but his crowning achievement is a canned yogurt. Simon, on the other hand, is involved in action, adventure, great risks, and great payoffs. Simon represents the last gasp of adventure in an increasingly tamed world.

The one question that Lelouch evades in the film concerns the morality of his hero. Is Simon a totally sympathetic figure, or does he have the ruthlessness of the traditional gangster? The kidnapping of the boy is not a particularly heinous act because of the father's connivance and the bank's cynicism and dishonesty. Young Daniel has a far better time with his kidnappers than with his parents, anyway. At other times, though, the crooks do commit violent acts: Simon forces Danièle Delorme's cooperation at knifepoint, and Charlot shoots up a police car. Does the filmmaker condone these acts? Lelouch ducks the moral problem by keeping his film light, fast-paced, and entertaining, and by minimizing the damage done by the gangsters. However, similar problems recur in later Lelouch films, especially *Cat and Mouse* (1975) and *The Good and the Bad* (1976).

Smic, Smac, Smoc (1971)

Smic, Smac, Smoc is a kind of film experiment, a return to Lelouch's roots in amateur filmmaking. It was shot in eight days on a budget of

$40,000 to test a new Eclair lightweight 16mm camera. Eighteen friends and associates of the director worked on the film, doubling as actors and technical crew. Lelouch's brief script outline, written just before production started, was elaborated by director and actors each day. *Smic* was then blown up to 35 mm and released as a normal film. It played at the 1971 Venice Film Festival and was a fair commercial success in France.

The film is about three workers in the shipyard of La Ciotat, near Marseilles, played by Charles Gérard, Jean Collomb, and Amidou. Their nicknames are derived from the SMIC (Salaire Minimum Interprofessionel de Croissance), the French minimum wage. The slim plot has Amidou marrying Catherine Allegret, who works in a bakery. The friends celebrate with a hillside picnic and hire blind accordionist Francis Lai to provide music. Then, on an impulse, they steal a car and drive to Saint-Tropez, where they dine at Byblos, an extremely fashionable, expensive, and stuffy restaurant. The clash of cultures in this scene resembles a Marx brothers movie, with Charles Gérard as Groucho. In the film's epilogue we see the main characters at a police station, arrested for "borrowing" the car and also a new accordion for Lai. "We didn't mean any harm," they lamely explain.

Smic is a populist film, a romanticized version of the working class. Unlike the troubled Parisians, the workers are poor but happy. They live very simply in the lush surroundings of the Mediterranean coast. The film also extends *The Crook's* theme of friendship; the Smicards are a close-knit group, not isolated individuals. The most important scene in this romantic vision is the picnic on the grass, which suggests (in the tradition of Renoir *père et fils*) a profound union between man and nature. The accordionist "makes up" a lovely song to commemorate the occasion:

> Ils étaient trois
> Mais trois c'est bien assez
> Quand c'est Smic, Smac, Smoc
>
> Qui travaillaient, dormaient, et travaillaient
> Faisaient cric, crac, croc . . .*

The song, the accordion, the rustic picnic, and the characters singing along all evoke a traditional, pastoral France, the France of René Clair or Marcel Pagnol.

Politically, the film is certainly not a workingman's manifesto. Though the workers are simpler and less pretentious than the bourgeoisie, their

*"Smic, Smac, Smoc," words by Catherine Desage, music by Francis Lai, © 1971 by Editions 23. Reprinted by permission of Editions 23 and Francis Lai.

desire is to go to Saint-Tropez and live like rich bourgeois. Political consciousness is minimal; Charlot rails about revolution only to get a better price from a shopkeeper. Further, the scene at the police station presents our heroes as lovable but irresponsible. Lelouch gently satirizes both the bourgeoisie and the working class.

Smic's great strength lies in the intimate observation of the characters and their world. The 16 mm camera is even more informal, more maneuverable than Lelouch's normal camera. He takes advantage of its light weight (only seven pounds) to shoot in long sequence shots, following the improvised action as it develops. This stylistic choice emphasizes the community of characters and the interplay between characters and environment. Also, the photography is so simple that when Lelouch produces an "effect"—for example, a love scene at night against a deep blue sky—it has a striking impact. Another informal technique the film uses quite well is oral titles—the simplest and most personal solution, but one that is almost never used. Charles Gérard's closing statement (substituting for the more common closing title), which suggests that if the spectator does not like the ending he should invent another one, is a hilarious example of what this technique can do.

The film's informality does have weaknesses. The plot is minimal, and the nonprofessional actors have trouble working together and filling in scenes where nothing much happens. So, there are many awkward moments. Charles Gérard's response to the thin plot and absence of ensemble play is to dominate most scenes with a steady stream of wisecracks. Still, there is a crazy charm in watching actors who have only half-absorbed their roles, and who are obviously having a good time. The good humor of the filming situation merges with the good humor of the filmed situation, and adds to the themes of simplicity and friendship.

Money, Money, Money (*L'Aventure c'est l'aventure*, 1972)

Money, Money, Money is about five "voyous" instead of one. It begins by introducing the heroes at work: Lino (Lino Ventura), Aldo (Aldo Maccione), Simon (Charles Denner), Jacques (Jacques Brel), and Charlot (Charles Gérard). We then see a period in which the criminal world is confused: Lino and Aldo have to contend with a prostitute's revolt; Jacques and Charlot pull a daring holdup and find no money in the till. Further, Lino's son is arrested for political, not criminal, reasons. When the five meet to play poker, Simon explains that the others are twenty years out of date. The big money is now in politics; he himself does very well wounding political targets for cash. Simon suggests that they study politics and go into political crime.

Money, Money, Money—The five crooks: Lino Ventura, Aldo Maccione, Charles Gérard, Charles Denner, Jacques Brel. (Academy of Motion Picture Arts and Sciences)

We next see a montage of lectures given by various political types to our heroes. The gangsters are thoroughly confused by dialectics, Trotskyism, and the like. Simon tells them that since they have understood nothing, they can stay above politics and make a lot of money.

Our heroes proceed to pull one astounding crime after another. They kidnap Johnny Hallyday (France's version of Elvis Presley) from an outdoor rock concert. They clean out a safe by masquerading as policemen. They kidnap a Swiss ambassador in South America on behalf of a guerrilla group.[4] When double-crossed by the guerrillas, they kidnap the Che-like leader, Ernesto Juarez, and sell him simultaneously to the guerrillas, the CIA, And a Latin American army. Two of them hijack a luxury airliner while two of the others are waiting at an insurance executive's office to negotiate a ransom.

While vacationing in the Caribbean, our heroes are once again captured by the guerrillas. After being tortured, they reveal the number of their Swiss bank account, and are then turned over to the French police. At trial, their attorney successfully portrays them as revolutionaries, and thus their confinement becomes embarrassing to the French government. They escape as the result of some ministerial politics.

Landing in Africa, the five gangsters are met with wild applause and celebration. They address a massive crowd with such varied slogans as "Power is at the end of a gun," "Politics is show business," and "I have a red convertible for sale." Each slogan gets equal applause. In Africa the five carry out their biggest project yet, the kidnapping of the Pope. The credits at the end of the film describe future projects: Nixon, Mao, Cassius Clay (later Muhammad Ali), and various French film personalities.

At Cannes, where *Money, Money, Money* was shown out of competition on opening night, Lelouch introduced it like this:[5] "I made this film because every morning, after reading the newspapers, I am totally confused. Our world has become crazy-crazy-crazy. So I made a crazy-crazy-crazy film. Something like 'Les Pieds-Nickelés 1972.'"* On another occasion he commented that *Money, Money, Money* was "a political film that I will treat in the form of derision."[6] Politics is so crazy that it can only be looked at from a comic and satiric distance.

The world of this film is even more corrupt than that of *The Crook*. Most of the people encountered by the gang are dishonest, immoral, and hypocritical. Johnny Hallyday pays for his own kidnapping as a publicity stunt. The ambassador's wife watches herself make a tearful plea on television, and then turns off the television to embrace her longhaired boyfriend. Ernesto Juarez thinks nothing of lying, cheating, and torturing for the sake of revolution. The French government is more influenced by political expediency and factional infighting than by justice.

The five gangsters are quite sympathetic in this context. None of them is a superman, either physically or intellectually; instead, they are all simple, warm human beings like the workers of *Smic, Smac, Smoc*. The disorientation of their profession reflects rapid changes throughout society. In turning to political crime, the five gangsters are not being cynical, but struggling to reduce a changed reality to something they can understand. Aldo, the dumbest of them, has never even heard of the Fifth (Republic), the C.G.T. (France's largest labor union), or the General (de Gaulle), and the others are not much better informed. Instead of learning politics, they work in it and judge it by the values of gangsterism: money, adventure, group solidarity, honor among thieves. The warm and humorous camaraderie of the crooks has a strong appeal in an unfriendly and incomprehensible world.

The film has the simple logic of the best satire: one starts from an outrageous yet plausible premise and extends it to the greatest possible enormity or absurdity. Each episode becomes progressively wilder and more shocking, but without becoming totally implausible. In fact, several situations shown in the film have become common occurrences *since* 1972: political meetings of prostitutes, political gunmen who

*"Les Pieds Nickelés": Slapstick characters from a well-known comic book. Their most important characteristic is a wacky inventiveness, an ability to get out of impossible situations.

wound their victims, a blurring of the line between revolutionary and criminal activity. The kidnapping of the Pope is a logical culmination to the series, since the Pope is a taboo personage supposedly above politics but who will certainly generate a huge ransom.*

The structure of more and more daring crimes has some interesting formal consequences. First, the narrative can be simple and direct. Lelouch has no need here for the subjectivity of *Life, Love, Death* or the tricks of *The Crook;* as he says, *Money, Money, Money* is *Smic* on a much larger scale.[7] Second, the meaning of the film lies in the intellectual concepts of the various crimes, in the spectator's recognition that each is outrageous but possible. Therefore, the process of each crime need not be shown; a few striking details will do. For example, Johnny Hallyday's kidnapping is shown by some footage of the concert, with our heroes fighting through the crowd, and then a scene of Johnny chatting with the gang about publicity and the ransom. The spectator fills in the blanks.

This elliptical approach to action leaves Lelouch free to develop his group of characters. Politics is confusing, but the group is simple and concrete. The characters are in robust health,[8] and they take nothing seriously—neither themselves, nor their jobs, nor outside authority. They often seem more like adolescents fooling around than like criminals. All of them are a bit eccentric (Simon is very nervous, Jacques is headstrong, and so on), but that adds to the comic flair of the group. Lelouch gave the actors considerable leeway here, as he did in *Smic, Smac, Smoc,* and with professionals the results are better. The actors are witty, relaxed, and comfortable with each other. They take full advantage of the comic possibilities of verbal repartee and ensemble play (both of which are lacking in Lelouch's earlier montage films). Ventura is especially good; frustrated and tense in the beginning, he becomes wonderfully relaxed and smooth as the gang's fortunes prosper. Once known strictly as a tough guy, Ventura expanded his range to light comedy and romance with this film and Lelouch's *Happy New Year* (1973).

As in *Smic,* the high point of *Money, Money, Money* has nothing at all to do with the plot. Instead, it involves our heroes' attempt to pick up some bikini-clad girls in the Caribbean. Aldo, the most childlike of the five, teaches the others in the group a sexy walk that can only be called the "Italian strut." One bends over, swings one's arms, and exaggerates

---

*The shooting of Pope John Paul II on May 13, 1981, suggests once again the anticipatory quality of Lelouch's satire. It also brings up troubling questions of artistic responsibility. Is there a possible relationship between Lelouch's film and real acts of terrorism, including the attack on the Pope? Is the film irresponsible in plot or in tone? International terrorists would certainly exist with or without Lelouch, but perhaps by poking fun at terrorism the film director has to some extent humanized it.

Money, Money, Money—The "Italian strut." (Academy of Motion Picture Arts and Sciences)

each movement in a caricature of a nonchalant, self-confident walk. Lelouch shows us each crook in turn parading his own variation on the strut. The girls seem only mildly amused. This scene, a comedy classic, demonstrates better than any narrative episode the innocence and good spirits of the heroes.

The film leaves itself open to at least two widely divergent interpretations. On the one hand, it could be called "The Revenge of the Silent Majority." We see five sympathetic, average Frenchmen (who happen to be crooks), bewildered and angry about political confusion and rapid social change. They decide to use the new political tactics while sticking to traditional values such as "work should be paid for" and "just do your job, don't worry about the rest." This is a clever way to get even with the new order while pointing up its absurdities. The conservative thrust of the argument is best seen in Lino's confrontation with his son. The son explains that capitalism and the consumer society are dead. Lino responds by blowing up his son's car with a conveniently available Molotov cocktail. But instead of thanking his father, the son calls him a fascist. The middle-class, middle-aged man thus shows up the contradictions of the new politics with plain common sense. Similarly, the consistent, old-fashioned crooks win our sympathies throughout the film.

On the other hand, the film can be seen as a satire of current politics that favors no group and suggests no solution. Underlying all the high spirits is a pessimistic view of society breaking down. Lelouch challenges us to find any difference between revolutionaries, government authorities, and the opportunistic crooks. The spectator is borne along by the logic and humor of the film, so that it takes an effort to stop and say, "No, this is all terribly wrong. Both the crooks and the others are wrong."

This divergence of meaning is probably the most interesting thing about *Money, Money, Money*. One laughs, but one also feels uneasy. The merry adventures of the gangsters are also a description of corruption on a colossal scale. The film is certainly not perfect. For example, Lelouch's businessmen are more convincing than his guerrillas, and he distorts an important problem by suggesting that torture can be funny (Aldo enjoys having a scorpion on his genitals). Still, the film does manage to be both a popular comedy and a wide-reaching satire.

Happy New Year (*La Bonne Année*, 1973)

Happy New Year is, first of all, about an ingenious jewel robbery. Simon (Lino Ventura) and Charles (Charles Gérard) arrive at the Carlton Hotel in Cannes to knock off the Van Cleef and Arpels jewelry store across the street. Simon visits the store disguised as a very old and wealthy man to win the manager's confidence. He declares on his return that he will pull the first "psychological" heist; the manager's greed will be his downfall. In the next few days the "old man" makes several more visits to Van Cleef, becoming a valued customer.

Meanwhile, Simon has noticed the beautiful Françoise (Françoise Fabian) who owns the antique store next to the jewelers'. He contrives to meet her through buying and selling an antique table, and they get along well. Simon's first clumsy attempt at seduction is rebuffed, but the couple meets again at Mass on Christmas Eve. At dinner afterwards, Françoise's intellectual friends offend Simon. He storms out, but she sends everyone home, including her lover, and calls Simon at the hotel. They sleep together.

The next day, Simon and Charles rob the jewelry store.* The old man plays on the manager's greed to get into the store after hours. Everything goes according to plan and Charles makes a daring escape

*Yes, Van Cleef and Arpels seems to be open on Christmas Day.

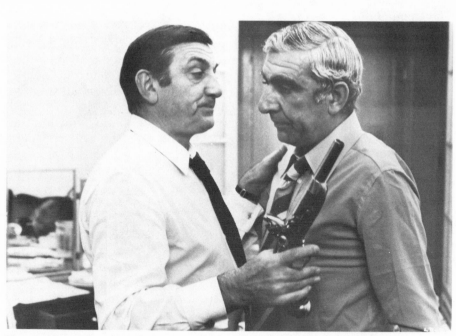

Happy New Year—Lino Ventura, Charles Gérard, and the "authentic Louis XVI" pistol. (Avco Embassy)

Happy New Year—Lino Ventura (in disguise) and Françoise Fabian. (Academy of Motion Picture Arts and Sciences)

with the loot, but Simon is caught because of a safety feature of which he was unaware. He surrenders to the police as Françoise watches.

This story, shown in color, is a long flashback surrounded by a framing story in black-and-white. The film begins in prison, where *A Man and a Woman* is shown to the inmates. After the movie, Simon finds he has been pardoned for the New Year (and, as we learn later, so the police can get a line on the jewel robbery). Simon goes to his Paris apartment, where Françoise has been living. He discovers, without letting anyone know of his presence, that she has another, younger lover. Simon glumly celebrates the New Year in a nightclub, Chez Michou. The film flashes back six years at this point.

After the flashback, Simon escapes his police tail and goes to meet Charles. They embrace. The next day Simon is at the airport, planning to fly to Brazil. At the last moment, he calls Françoise. Although she is in bed with her lover, she says to Simon, "My love, where are you? Come quickly." Simon arrives at the apartment and stares gloomily across the table, remembering the other man. The film ends as Simon finally says, "Happy New Year. I'll have coffee now."

Lelouch, who was very pleased with *Happy New Year*, says it is the first film that combines his three major themes: love, action, and friendship.[9] Both a gangster film and a love story, it is a kind of summary of Lelouch's career to date. It is also a film about happiness, as love, action, and friendship all come together in Simon's life, at least for a moment.[10] Combining the three themes gives a picture of a complete personality.

With the daring crime, Simon and Charles establish once again the superiority of the independent gangster figure over a passive and mediocre society. Following the tradition of the "caper movie," Lelouch shows us the planning and execution of the robbery in great detail so that we can empathize with the skill and courage of the heroes. The method used is "psychology," not violence; as in *The Crook*, Simon exploits the weaknesses and vices of his victims. Here the specific targets are the manager's obsequious greed plus the safe and respectable environment of the store, which makes robbery unthinkable. To some extent the crime is motivated by social class. Simon and Charles, upwardly mobile from the working class, attack a symbol of bourgeois prestige and respectability.

Just as important as the robbery itself is the rapport between the crooks. The shared adventure of crime produces a close and humorous camaraderie between them. Their dialogue often consists of a series of witty retorts. Simon laughs at Charles for being slow and dense, and Charles punctures Simon's big ideas with a rude common sense. Underlying the good-natured quarrels is a great deal of warmth and mutual

respect. In fact, the relationship is so close that Simon's reunion with
Charles on New Year's Eve is the most emotional moment of the film.

At first, the love story is just an added consequence of Simon's good
spirits while planning the crime. He sees Françoise while he is watching
Van Cleef's, and as a man of action he decides to pursue her. For a short
time, two ingenious plots are going on at the same time—the robbery of
Van Cleef's and the seduction of the antique dealer. However, the
courtship soon becomes more than a pursuit as Françoise proves to be
Simon's equal—intelligent, independent, and unpredictable.

Much of the love story revolves around how different the two characters are. The gangster is once again the traditionalist. Simon, the
straightforward man of action, unconcerned with appearances and social
nuances, seems out of place in fashionable, mannered Cannes. He lives
by a simple moral code: independence, pride in workmanship, loyalty to
friends. He is a marginal character by social class and occupation. Françoise, on the other hand, is a liberated modern woman, "a woman who
lives like a man," says Simon. She runs a successful, high-status business
and is very much a part of her society. She is also an intellectual, one
who sees the world in complex terms.

The meeting of these two characters requires compromise on both
sides. Françoise must forget her familiar, comfortable life-style and her
intellectual pretensions to bet on an uncultured but vigorous stranger.
Simon must accept that Françoise is an independent person, and therefore change his behavior and values accordingly. Françoise's compromise is glossed over, but Simon's struggle to change is central to the
film. The entire framing story is about the painfulness of this struggle,
made more poignant by memories of a simpler, happier time (the robbery). The film ends without giving us any assurance that Simon can
adapt.

Happy New Year can be seen as both a summary and a revision of
Lelouch's earlier work. The opening reference to *A Man and a Woman*,
which is booed by the convicts, suggests that that film too simply and
neatly resolves the problems of the couple.[11] Although it has flashes of
the earlier film's lyricism, the love story in *Happy New Year* is more
problematic and complex. Instead of relying on an emotional montage,
the film presents two charming, articulate characters who are not necessarily made for each other. The greatest single change from the earlier
film lies in the independence of the female character. In all his films
since *L'Amour avec des si* (an interesting exception), Lelouch's women
are passive, emotional, and dependent on men. Françoise in *Happy
New Year* remains an attractive and desirable woman, but she has the
self-reliance and spirit to take care of herself. This makes romantic
relationships more complicated and perhaps more satisfying; it also

changes the behavior of the male. Lelouch has returned to the figure of the independent woman in several films after *Happy New Year*.

The film can also be seen as a revision of Lelouch's gangster-adventure films. In *The Crook* and *Money, Money, Money*, the adventures are a comic fantasy of mastering an unfriendly world. *Happy New Year* looks at the disjunction between crook and society in a more realistic vein. Here the joy of adventure remains, but instead of laughing at the world, the crook realizes that he is lonely, getting old, and out of step with the times. The man of action is faced with the necessity of compromise and change.

At some point during the early 1970s, Lelouch became an excellent director of actors. He no longer cuts up performances into small fragments, depending solely on the actor's visual expression. Instead, *Happy New Year* features many long sequence shots for both action scenes and conversations. In the dialogue scenes, camera work enhances the verbal sparring of the actors, rather than overwhelming it. For example, the playfully philosophical dialogue that truly introduces the couple takes place on a walk through Cannes; movement, light, and setting add to the quiet lyricism of the scene. Part of the change in style is the result of the use of a new lightweight 35 mm camera, the Arriflex BL, which Lelouch now uses on all his films. Equally important is a new attitude toward acting. Since *Smic*, Lelouch has encouraged spontaneity not only by surprising his actors but by giving them the opportunity to stretch out and relax in long takes. The technique works very well in this film. The acting in the flashback section is a bit larger than life, expressing the characters' health and joie de vivre. In the framing story, the actors are quieter, more reserved, and a bit strained. These dynamics are more subtle and consistent than in Lelouch's earlier films.

The three main roles are extremely well cast and well performed. Lino Ventura, too old, too fat, and too grim to be a leading man in a conventional love story, manages to be charming and witty while retaining hints of a tough pessimism. His disguise, the rich old gentleman, shows just how resourceful he can be. Ventura masters a complex role with ease; clearly, this actor has many talents. Françoise Fabian's role is very similar to her performance in Eric Rohmer's *My Night at Maud's*: an independent, frank, but also mysterious woman. In Rohmer's film she dominates an indecisive Jean-Louis Trintignant; in Lelouch's film she has the strength to match a powerful performance by Ventura. Though overshadowed by the other actors, Charles Gérard still turns in a fine performance. Playing one of those rare characters who is totally eccentric yet totally healthy and functioning. Gérard's interaction with Ventura softens and humanizes the film's main character.

One index of Lelouch's workmanship in *Happy New Year* is a symbolic coherence that is not often found in his films. Consider, for example, this chain of relationships: Françoise is interested in antiques, and thus in the backward-looking Simon. They meet because of a Louis XVI table by Nicolas Cochin, whom Françoise describes as "the enemy of rococo, of the palm, of the acanthus leaf . . . of all the decadent ornaments that characterize the style of Louis XV."[12] The classical Cochin equals the traditional Simon. As a further twist, Charles gives Simon an authentic Louis XVI pistol for Christmas. The gun is a reminder to avoid pretension, stick to business, and remember one's roots. These and other symbols in the film are playful, not arcane or "serious." They add to the film's warm and vigorous tone.

Happy New Year finds Lelouch acting like a genre filmmaker in a genre he has just invented: the comedy-gangster-adventure film with love story. He covers familiar material but adds new insights to it. The film is a kind of synthesis of Lelouch's work, a combination of his basic concerns in one simple pattern. Though not quite as original as *The Crook* and *Money, Money, Money*, this film is certainly thoughtful, well-made, and amusing.

Conclusions

Genre films were once regarded as inherently limited and demeaning. "Serious" filmmaking had nothing to do with the formula Western or gangster picture. However, in the last twenty to thirty years filmmakers and critics have recognized that the genre patterns offer certain advantages. They provide a kind of shorthand for getting at basic social issues within a simple but elegant form. The spectator following the logic of a genre story can easily grasp ideas that might be too complex or abstract if presented elsewhere. For example, the gangster film describes a conflict between individual initiative and social control. The gangster hero tests the limits of freedom and the consequences of law. This type of issue, which might be forbiddingly dry in other contexts, is made attractive and comprehensible by the genre's symbolic play. The genre pattern also imposes a discipline on the filmmaker, since he must work within a large body of conventions. Such discipline can be limiting, but in many cases it is actually helpful, because the conventional form requires structure and coherence. Creativity is not destroyed but channeled. The filmmaker's job is to transform the already existing elements of the genre into his own unique and meaningful synthesis.

Lelouch is not usually regarded as a genre director, but he has done much of his best work in the gangster or crime film.[13] Along with Melville, Chabrol, Godard, Truffaut, and (in another genre) Sergio

Leone, Lelouch has absorbed the lessons of American genre filmmaking and recast them to his own requirements. In the four films from *The Crook* (1970 to *Happy New Year* (1973), Lelouch's theme is the joyous activity of the crook juxtaposed with the mediocrity of the surrounding society. He makes his heroes very sympathetic to bring out the virtues of individualism, such as independence, toughness, and friendship. These characters are struggling with all their skill, strength, and intelligence to retain dignity and freedom of action. A society in decay makes them all the more appealing. Lelouch does not stress the limits of freedom, although the Smicards must pay for their crimes and the hero of *Happy New Year* is seen as anachronistic and incomplete. The director is more interested in crime as a metaphor for threatened individualism.

The light, comic manner of these films has a few different functions. First, it creates a distance between spectator and genre, and thus points to the metaphor Lelouch wants to get across. The comic adventures of the heroes bring up questions like "What is crime? What is adventure?" Second, the comic tone approximates the joys and marvelous successes of the characters. Empathizing with the hero, the viewer shares the pleasures of action. Third, the tone is clearly a way to keep the spectator's interest. Lelouch makes rather thoughtful films in the guise of pleasant genre entertainments. His films may even be too pleasant, thus muting their critical aspect.

Lelouch attributes his change in style, from the subjectivity and sentimentality of *A Man and a Woman* or *Life, Love, Death* to the irony and greater objectivity of *The Crook*, to a concern for the audience and his own maturation. He says, "The public wants a story, always, always, always,"[14] and, therefore, Lelouch turned from aesthetic and technical interests to a simpler storytelling. Lelouch comments about maturity that "when one is very young one takes everything seriously, one speaks seriously. But the great quality of age is precisely that it gives you a philosophy which takes things with much more humor."[15] The subjectivity of *A Man and a Woman* treats a shake of Anouk's head or a movement of Jean-Louis's car with tremendous gravity. It presents an intense tunnel vision. The ironic storytelling of *The Crook* or *Money, Money, Money* allows Lelouch a more global vision. He can observe and poke fun at an entire society using the genre form.

The change in style does involve a certain price. The subjective films are all to some extent experimental works, film poems. The crime films, on the other hand, work through more conventional narratives. So, Lelouch has lost some of the lyrical freedom of his early works. But the change to genre narratives is also a significant gain for him. The crime film pattern gives a direction to his thinking, and thus eliminates much of the awkwardness of the earlier films. It also provides a basis for

multileveled filmmaking. Each film of this period is enjoyable as an
adventure story, a character study, an homage to the genre, the evocation of a mood, the sketch of a social problem.

Lelouch's fluency in the crime genre is remarkable. He draws on
varied elements of the genre like the gangster, the conman, the big
caper, the prison film, and even the juvenile delinquent (the Smicards
are more delinquent than criminal) to create a group of films that are
related but also distinct from one another. The themes of individualism,
action, and friendship are constant in the series, but specific films explore topical issues like publicity *(The Crook)*, populism *(Smic)*, and
political terrorism *(Money, Money, Money)*. And, although the series
begins by breaking with sentimentality, by the time of *Happy New Year*
Lelouch has recombined a love story with the crime film plot. Lelouch
seems capable of doing almost anything in the crime genre.

5
Un Chef d'Oeuvre Manqué

And Now My Love (*Toute une vie*, 1974)

The commercial and critical success of *Happy New Year* encouraged Lelouch to go ahead with his most ambitious project, *And Now My Love* (*Toute une vie*, 1974). He had been planning this film, originally called *Toute la vie d'un homme*, for ten years or more. The idea for the film always had an epic scope; in 1967 Lelouch described it as "the film of my career."[1] The film was originally planned as the story of a man from his birth to his death. The final conception was expanded quite a bit: it includes not only the story of a filmmaker who resembles Lelouch, but also a female protagonist, three generations of her family, a history of cinema, and a panorama of world events in the twentieth century.

Lelouch shot the film in eighteen weeks (a normal film takes him six to eight weeks) on location in France, Italy, Moscow, Hong Kong, Israel, Kenya, Rio de Janeiro, the United States, and Turkey. The budget for the film was about $6 million, routine for Hollywood in the 1970s but very high for a French film, which cannot cover this kind of budget unless it is a large international success. Lelouch notes that the film would have cost much more if it were made as a standard, big-company production.[2] Instead, the director traveled with a small crew (thirteen people for his trip around the world),[3] held the camera himself, and worked sixteen hours a day. Lelouch lost twenty pounds while shooting the film.

And Now My Love is a very large and complicated film: one hundred years, a dozen main characters, and hundreds of scenes are compressed into two and a half hours in the French version of the film, two hours in the American version. For convenience of analysis, we divide the film into three parts, corresponding to the past, present, and future. The future section, a flashforward, exists only in the French version of the film; for the other sections we refer to the American version.

79

1900–1946

The first part of the film juxtaposes personal joy and sorrow with the great events of the century. It begins on a Paris street in 1900. A movie cameraman (Charles Denner) invites a young woman (Judith Magre) to try his camera: "It's an invention with a future," he says. This little scene, shown in black and white with titles to imitate the silent films, brings together the paternal grandparents of Sarah Goldman, the heroine of the film. It also begins Lelouch's history of the cinema, and it introduces a happy, nostalgic tune that will recur several times.

Lelouch presents World War I in one long take. A messenger goes down an extremely long trench to the photographer shown in the previous scene, operating his camera at the front. The photographer opens his letter, shouts, "It's a boy!," and is immediately blown up by an explosion. When the smoke clears, the French army charges over the spot where the photographer had just stood. The long take here shows the tremendous gap between individuals and large-scale events that characterizes *And Now My Love*.

After a light romantic interlude involving a chorus girl (Marthe Keller), a general (Daniel Boulanger), and the general's adjutant (Yvan Tanguy), the film cuts to a sequence of newsreels: first, silent newsreel shots of Lenin, Trotsky, and Stalin; then, the Warner Brothers sound short of Will Hays, in which he says, "The movies are beginning to talk"; then, sound newsreel footage of Adolf Hitler. This sequence has multiple meanings, but it is mainly a way to displace the individual story with weighty historical events as World War II approaches. The sober tone of the newsreels alludes to the coming tragedy of war.

We return to the individual story on a train bringing survivors of the concentration camps back to France. On this train, David Goldman (Charles Denner), the son of the photographer, meets Rachel Stern (Marthe Keller), the daughter of the chorus girl. When we next see them, in Paris, the film's cinematography switches from black-and-white to color. The formal change corresponds to the marriage of David and Rachel, the liberation of Paris, and the introduction of color in the French film industry. However, the union of individual and collective happiness is very brief. Rachel dies giving birth to a daughter, Sarah, and a long close-up shows David facing the news alone in a hospital corridor. Sarah will write in her diary that her mother, weakened by the camp, was a delayed victim of World War II. Thus, the lessons of World War I—man's isolation, and the tragic effects of world events on the individual—are repeated.

The film's opening section, about half an hour long, shows how the human comedy of birth, death, love, grief, and pleasure survives even

And Now My Love—Charles Denner and Marthe Keller. Returning from the concentration camps. (Academy of Motion Picture Arts and Sciences)

in the most tragic times. Its rapid, clever montage evokes a series of moods while giving a very simple picture of history and the individual. Many scenes are distanced by pantomime, editing tricks, and the nostalgic little theme, creating the comic effect, but there are a few moments of intense emotion. The most striking is the meeting of David and Rachel, the rebirth of life after a horrible war. Though beautifully photographed, edited, and scored, this part of the film is not complete in itself. It is rather, an evocative, impressionistic prologue to the main action.

1962–1974

The middle section of the film, 1962–1974, is too intricate to summarize scene by scene. It tells the parallel stories of Sarah Goldman (Marthe Keller), the daughter of David and Rachel, and Simon Duroc (André Dussolier), a young thief who becomes a film director. These two characters are linked by a long series of experiences, coincidences, tastes, and superstitions. Some of the connections are quite complex. For example, after Simon cracks up a car in escaping from prison, we cut to a hospital where Sarah is recuperating from a suicide attempt. Meanwhile, a newsman (Gérard Sire) announces that "the death of Marilyn

And Now My Love—Marthe Keller and Gilbert Bécaud. The sixteenth-birthday party. (Avco Embassy)

Monroe marks the end of the affluent society," and we hear a few bars of "Bye, Bye, Baby" (sung by Monroe). The whole passage describes a loss of innocence. Other connections are trivial: Simon and Sarah both take three lumps of sugar in their coffee, and their astrological signs are complementary. The film also refers to the great events of 1962–74: the death of John Kennedy, the war in Vietnam, the French elections of 1965, the Arab-Israeli War of 1967, May 1968 in France, the moon landing, and others. However, world history stays in the background in this part of the film.

The narrative concentrates slightly more on Sarah, the poor little rich girl. She is introduced by a montage of birthday parties. David Goldman now owns a successful shoe factory, so with each party his house gets larger and Sarah's gift becomes more lavish. For her sixteenth birthday, Sarah gets Gilbert Bécaud, the French pop star, who sings for the party and then seduces her. She falls hard for Bécaud, but he drops her. This is Sarah's first indication that the glamorous illusions of publicity and fashion do not correspond to reality.

Sarah goes through all the misadventures of her generation: pot parties, sexual permissiveness, travel and idleness, a six-day marriage, an experiment with socialism. All of her experiences leave her basically untouched except for the death of her father, which recapitulates the film's theme that intimate relationships are precious and irreplaceable.

Sarah glides through life, vivacious but without purpose.* She enjoys the pleasures of wealth, but feels vaguely dissatisfied. The dynamic and extremely gifted Marthe Keller beautifully captures Sarah's appetite for life and her confusion. She makes us believe that Sarah is a person of great potential despite the superficiality of her life-style.

Sarah's attitude toward men is an interesting mixture of active and passive. On the one hand, she dominates some of the men in her life. Her lover Jean, for example, is treated simply as a convenience. Sarah writes in her diary that he has the virtues and faults of an obedient dog. She is also very aggressive with her husband, with a union leader she dates, and with a "stud" she picks up on the street. On the other hand, Sarah and her father are both convinced that the right man ("l'homme de ta vie") will solve all her problems. In a sense, she spends the entire film waiting for that man. After *Happy New Year*, it seems strange that the option of an independent, self-reliant woman is not explored in *And Now My Love*. But perhaps the difference between films is more apparent than real; Françoise Fabian also has one "man of her life."

Simon is introduced to us in the process of stealing a Bécaud album, as Bécaud's song "Voleur d'Oranges" plays on the sound track. Simon is a poor orphan, a man with no history. He lives alone in an apartment crammed with stolen consumer goods. Simon's illusions crack when he is caught and sent to jail. In prison, however, he finds a father figure, Sam (Sam Letrone), a friend, Charlot (Charles Gérard), and a profession (photography). On his release, Simon goes from photography to porno films to commercials and then to feature films. Happy in his work, his only problem is loneliness in his personal life. Despite Charlot's companionship, Simon drifts through glamorous Paris.

Simon is a combination of Lelouch's gangster-hero with a self-portrait of the director. Daring self-reliant crook equals daring self-reliant filmmaker; the connection was already implicit in the earlier films and explicit in some of the things written about Lelouch.[4] Simon's criminal background shows that he started from nothing and that he is willing to take risks. Prison is also a metaphor for loneliness. The film's biographical aspect is more elaborate. Simon's career closely parallels Lelouch's, and films like *A Man and a Woman*, *Grenoble*, and *Life, Love, Death* are specifically referred to. At the end of the film Simon is actually preparing an *And Now My Love*–like film. Lelouch also uses Simon's career to comment on *Cahiers du Cinéma*, pornography, and his critics.

*Sarah does find a cause to work for in the French version of the film. Following her father's deathbed wish, she goes to Israel to fight in the 1974 Yom Kippur War. Both the flashback to the deathbed and the scene of Sarah in Israel were cut from the American version. This subplot makes Sarah's trip to New York "for Israel" at the end of the film comprehensible, and it presents Sarah as a more complete, more attractive person. It does not, however, drastically change the film.

And Now My Love—André Dussolier as the crook who becomes a film director. (Academy of Motion Picture Arts and Sciences)

And Now My Love—Marthe Keller as the poor little rich girl. (Academy of Motion Picture Arts and Sciences)

And Now My Love is Lelouch's film about filmmaking; however, it lacks the intensity of the two modern masterworks on the subject, *Day for Night* and *8½*. Lelouch may have erred in casting Dussolier, who played the hapless sociologist in Truffaut's *Such a Gorgeous Kid like Me*, as Simon. Dussolier is a sensitive actor, but he does not have the conviction and inner strength one would expect of a film director.*

The present section of the film ends very traditionally. Simon and Sarah break with their daily lives and take a plane to New York. After a parallel montage of them leaving home, driving to the airport, and checking their baggage, they meet at long last on the plane. The meeting does not need to be shown in great detail, because it has been so carefully prepared. The last shot of the film (in both versions) shows the lovers' symbolic coupling. Their two suitcases, which went up the conveyer belt side by side at Orly, come off the plane in New York one on top of the other (naturally, Simon's is on top). The scene, shot from below, emphasizes the birth imagery of the suitcases coming out of the airplane. Meanwhile, the nostalgic little tune that accompanied the meeting of Sarah's grandparents in 1900 returns on the sound track. The meeting of the couple reaffirms the value of romantic love and thus resolves, at least for the moment, all the problems of the film. Simon gets Sarah, and Sarah gets Simon.

This section of *And Now My Love* is also very conservative politically. Though it shows a great diversity of actions and institutions, everything is slanted toward the status quo. At his Cannes press conference, Lelouch said that the film was based on the idea of contradiction, and that it went back and forth between Left and Right: "I affirm something, and, immediately afterwards, its opposite."[5] Actually, though, the contradictions mainly undercut all threats to middle-class comfort and security. Socialism is brought up several times in the film, only to be belittled. A Marxist critique of Simon's first film becomes a burlesque, as Jacques Villeret wildly throws around words like "fascist" and "racist." A futurologist's warning on pollution is undercut because he chain smokes. The contrasting backgrounds of Simon and Sarah may be an attempt to show class differences, but here again Lelouch cheats. Simon is an orphan, with no traditions behind him, whereas Sarah has a history, a family, and an identity.[6] Further, Simon and Sarah learn exactly the same values from Sam and David, respectively. The two father figures agree on the necessity of capitalism, the virtues of the United States, and the nobility of gangsterism (as an extension of capitalism). This agreement makes the poor less threatening to the rich.

*A vignette from the film may describe the problems of directing one's own story: Simon, filming his autobiography, has great difficulty communicating his psychology and motivations to the actor playing his role. The actor is hesitant and unconvincing as Simon. Similarly, Simon is an inferior version of Lelouch.

The best that can be said of Lelouch's politics is that a margin of doubt remains. The very conservative David Goldman, who has a pithy saying for every situation, is the film's main political spokesman, but he is not necessarily the voice of Lelouch. Even David feels that his wealth is temporary: In 1962 he says, "There's fighting in Algeria, missiles in Cuba, a wall in Berlin. So who can expect much of the future?" Sarah and Simon live luxuriously but feel uneasy in a shallow modern world of chrome and glass and few personal relationships. Sarah often resists her father's advice, though she has no system to put in its place. Although the film's transcendent ending should solve all these problems, the ironic image of two suitcases on a conveyor belt suggests that some difficulties may remain.

1974–2000

The American version of *And Now My Love*, edited under the supervision of Joseph Levine, ends with the plane ride to New York and the last shot of the suitcases. The original, French version of the film also ends with the suitcases, but a long flashforward interrupts the airplane scene. Simon and Sarah's chat is interrupted by a montage of dates, 1974 to 1990, then a series of news announcements, in various languages, describing an ecological catastrophe. Monstrous babies are being born; sperm is polluted; a new type of cancer has appeared. Sex for reproduction is banned, as is artificial insemination. The end of the world has come.

We cut to Simon and Sarah, in flowing robes, watching television in their futuristic home. Sarah says, "I want a child." They visit a doctor and then go to a detoxification center, an isolated desert village that is unpolluted. Scenes at the detoxification center show them doing rhythmic exercises and dancing, along with many other couples. The exotic locale and the yellow robes worn by everyone give the center a religious aspect. Finally, one night an older man comes to tell the couple their child has been born. They watch their baby in a room full of incubators, an image of the survival of humanity.

We cut back to the plane, where Simon describes to Sarah this future segment of his planned film, where having children will be a problem. Meanwhile, Sarah talks about Israel. The flashforward is probably not a real future, but rather Simon's vision of his future life with Sarah. The distinction is important since, for one thing, the main characters have not aged in the flashforward.

The future scene was shot in central Turkey, in a remote village hewn out of a cliff. Although Lelouch was assisted by the Turkish government, the costs for cast, crew, electricity, and hundreds of extras must have been enormous. The results are uneven. Lelouch's panning camera and

Francis Lai's music combine with dancers, musicians, the exotic locale, and even flowing water for some strong, lyrical movements. However, the scene lacks authenticity and detail. The clearly ancient village does not correspond with the future setting, and little things are also wrong: musicians with electric instruments play with their feet in the water; Lai's themes do not match the rock musicians we see on screen. Further, the scene has neither a narrative nor a strong formal organization, so it drags.

By cutting out the sequence in the future, Joe Levine speeded up the film and eliminated one of its less successful parts. Still, one loses something with that cut. In the American ending the image of the suitcases has tremendous weight; it resolves and concludes the whole film. In the French version this image is not so awkwardly crammed with meaning. The suitcases become a clever joke because life continues, by flashforward, beyond them. The flashforward "ends" the film with a new twist on the theme that love is difficult, but possible.

And Now My Love attempts a synthesis far more ambitious than that of *Happy New Year*. It is not only an adventure-love story but also an autobiography, historical film, political film, and film about cinema. Unfortunately, Lelouch does not completely realize his grand design. He has problems with politics, with the future, and with dialogue. Lelouch has compared the film's varied contents to a restaurant menu;[7] one should add that the quality is extremely variable.

Despite its problems, though, the film does work very well as spectacle, as an emotional experience. Like *A Man and a Woman*, it combines striking montage with a strong musical score to present a memorable progression of emotions. The main themes are life, death, pleasure, happiness, and loneliness; the same themes as in the earlier film, but shown here with far more detail and self-assurance. Lelouch's technique has never been better; he creates a complex scene in just a few seconds, and then ingeniously cuts to another, equally interesting vignette. In fact, the film produces a kind of sensory overload; it is too rich in images and sounds to be fully grasped in one viewing. And where *A Man and a Woman* sustains a powerful montage construction for half an hour, *And Now My Love* cleverly combines emotional montage with more conventional narrative through the entire film.

And Now My Love is in many ways close to musical comedy. Although not in the usual form of the singing or dancing musical, it does have an elaborate score (Bécaud songs and Francis Lai orchestral pieces plus French and American pop songs of the century), singing, dancing, a choreographed camera, and the vivid, expressive images of the best film musicals. Bécaud, a tremendously dynamic performer, helps set the film's energetic tone. His songs continue on the sound track even after his dramatic role concludes. Marthe Keller adds another element: trained in ballet in her native Switzerland, she is an effervescent actress who can create a mood through movement and posture even when she is not dancing. She is beautifully showcased here in a triple role. The film also has a thematic resemblance to American musical comedy. In Lelouch's film, as in most musicals, the vital and spontaneous individual overcomes all inhibiting forces and finds love. *And Now My Love* could actually be seen as history critiqued by popular music.

The musical film seems to involve some inevitable simplification and stylization. Music, after all, is not as precise a form of communication as narrative, although it may say some things that narrative cannot. Not only the classic musicals, but also such modern hybrids as *Umbrellas of Cherbourg* and *Cabaret* greatly simplify narrative and setting to empha-size their musical elements. Lelouch refuses to do this in *And Now My Love*. He wants the lyricism of a musical plus the opportunity to com-ment, at length, on the twentieth century. However, an involuntary simplification occurs. Many topics are dealt with so briefly and schemat-ically that the film becomes clichéd. The musical-topical film for which Lelouch is striving may be possible, but he does not achieve it here.

The public reception of *And Now My Love* makes a fascinating story in itself. Lelouch opened the film out of competition at the Cannes Film Festival after a huge publicity campaign. Presented to an audience consisting mainly of journalists, the film was jeered and heckled through its second half. When Lelouch got on stage for a prearranged press conference, he was very angry. He accused the audience of not under-standing his film and not giving it a chance. "I had the impression during the projection," he said, "of being in a children's park watching a puppet show, and not with an audience of adults."[8]

Following this debacle the reviews of the film were overwhelmingly negative. Even critics who were generally favorable to Lelouch felt that *And Now My Love* was a failure. The French critics strongly objected to the film's politics, and especially to the dialogue given to Charles Den-ner. Their reaction might be related to the French presidential elections of 1974; the second and final round of the elections, in which Giscard d'Estaing defeated Mitterand by a margin of about 1 percent, took place on the same weekend that Lelouch presented his film at Cannes. In a highly charged political atmosphere, Lelouch's film, which takes politics lightly, may have offended an intellectual audience.[9] Strangely enough, *Money, Money, Money* had played to a similar Cannes audience in 1972 with no problems. Perhaps the humor of *Money, Money, Money* de-fused any criticism whereas the obvious sincerity of *And Now My Love* inflamed it.

The response of the French and European public at the box office was also very disappointing. Lelouch's most ambitious film became his biggest commercial failure, his only real failure since *Les Grands Moments*.

The American reaction to *And Now My Love* has been quite different. The film got rave reviews from several important critics, and it was voted the best foreign film of the year by the Los Angeles Film Critics' Association.[10] American critics in general were more interested in the virtues of the film as spectacle than in its politics or dialogue. Although it was never a big popular success, *And Now My Love* is still playing in art and repertory theaters in the United States, and it will probably be remembered here as one of the best French films of the 1970s.

6

Moral Realism, Genre Optimism

Le Mariage (1974)

June 1944. A young, working-class couple (Bulle Ogier and Rufus) buy a small cottage in Saint-Aubin-sur-Mer, Normandy. They are optimistic about living together in their new home even though it has no heat, no bathtub, faulty wiring, a window that won't open, and so on. Also, a German army blockhouse stands a few yards away. The young man carries his bride into the house on their wedding night. The next morning, the Resistance takes over the house at gunpoint, and uses it to assist the Allied invasion.

June 6, 1954. Rufus—now, unjustly, a Resistance hero—reads a speech on the tenth anniversary of the Allied landing to a crowd assembled in the town square. His wife and son watch the ineptly conducted local celebration. At home the couple's life is extremely strained. Ogier screams about all the problems with the house—none of the original defects has been repaired. Rufus is ambitious; he wants to be mayor of his village but he refuses to do anything to improve the comfort or well-being of his family—no eating out, no vacations, no television. Both parents are mean to their son. The conversations between Ogier and Rufus become more and more bitter (Sample dialogue: She: "We haven't made love in six months." He: "You can wait six more months!"), until he pushes her off the couch and she goes up to bed. Then he calls his mistress.

June 6, 1964. Rufus, now mayor of Saint-Aubin, gives the same speech he gave in 1954. His now teenage son wrecks the concluding "minute of silence" by revving his motorcycle as Ogier looks on approvingly. The house has still not been repaired, but the family does have a television. Husband and wife, no longer talking to each other, fall asleep in front of the set. Late at night the son comes home with another teenage boy; they sneak upstairs holding hands. Then the father sneaks downstairs to slash the tires on his son's motorcycle.

June 6, 1974. A different speaker addresses a small crowd in the town square. Meanwhile, a young couple walks up to the cottage, which is for sale. Ogier speaks about the cottage in the same terms as the woman who sold it to her: "We lived here happily for thirty years." All the original defects in the cottage still remain. In the evening Ogier watches television, gets a call from her son, and goes to bed. Then the camera walks down the street, in the house, up the stairs; we see the subjective viewpoint of someone walking, accompanied by footsteps and breathing. This person turns out to be Rufus, now a ragged bum, who has been living at a nearby hotel for a month. Ogier tells him that perhaps he shouldn't have come back home. Then she recalls the optimistic promises of their wedding night. "Do you remember?", she asks. The film ends.

Le Mariage, like *Smic, Smac, Smoc,* is an experimental film for Lelouch. He shot it in two weeks, on a very low budget, and tried out several new ideas. The film is a curious mixture of Lelouch's usual informality and a more intense, theatrical style. Both main actors have a background in "marginal" theater—Ogier in the avant-garde troupe of Marc'O, Rufus in one-man café-theater shows. Lelouch leaves them free to improvise their stormy interchanges, shooting in extremely long takes; Rufus says the director-cameraman often acted as a "simple reporter."[1] The resulting performances have a hysterical edge that is more typical of avant-garde theater than of the "cooler" medium of film. The use of one location, the interior and exterior of the cottage, and the many narrative repetitions add to a sense of theatrical enclosure. A further stylization is provided by the yellow tint of most of the film.* However, Lelouch's informal camera is as fluid as ever,and the uneven, spontaneous quality of the acting recalls his earlier films (especially *Smic*) as well as a certain theater. Lelouch begins the film very informally by speaking the credits, a device probably borrowed from Sacha Guitry, to whom *Le Mariage* is dedicated.

The film's bleak mood certainly sets it apart from Lelouch's earlier work. In *Life, Love, Death,* François Toledo has brief moments of happiness that suggest life's possibilities and counterpoint the horrors of capital punishment. In *Le Mariage,* however, Lelouch is savagely pessimistic about the couple's life together. In 1944 Ogier is a charming girl and Rufus is a shy young man, but ten years later the marriage is a trap for two people who hate each other. Although Ogier mentions divorce, it does not seem to be a real possibility in a small provincial town. So, man and wife endure their life together for thirty years. Hatred is finally replaced by a knowing resignation, rather than by any kind of hope. The yellow tint suggests the mediocrity of these lives.

*The last section, 1974, is in a more normal color, but is still heavily weighted toward yellow.

Rufus is the villain of the piece, an egotist and hypocrite who is constantly justifying himself. Though personally ambitious, he refuses to do anything to improve or change the family's life; change would be a sign of weakness. Instead, he takes great pleasure in imposing his will on those weaker than he, his wife and son. Lelouch very cleverly connects public and private hypocrisy by having the Rufus character capitalize on his false reputation as war hero. This suggests that business and politics and family are often mere facades concealing an empty, arid existence. Even as mayor of Saint-Aubin, Rufus is emotionally, spiritually, and morally bankrupt.

The Bulle Ogier character is a victim but also, to some extent, a coward. She knows the marriage is a trap, but her only responses are first, to complain, and second, to try to believe that her husband retains some shred of feeling toward her. With these attitudes, she goes from adolescence to nostalgia with nothing in between. The major failing of both characters is their lack of daring and imagination. Ogier feels that she should get out, perhaps go to Paris, but she never moves. When things go wrong she has no solution.

Lelouch admits that *Le Mariage* was to some extent a reaction to the poor critical and public reception of *And Now My Love*.[2] Since critics did not like the naive optimism of the earlier film, he gave them a bitter, depressing film that doubtless corresponded to his mood. His own marriage had broken up in the early 1970s, and this, too, must have contributed to the film's tone. We can also look at *Le Mariage* as Lelouch's fullest expression of contempt for the safe, passive life. In many of his films the presence of an exceptional hero or heroic group diffuses a criticism of the "average Frenchman" (which is what Ogier calls Rufus). In *The Crook*, for example, Simon the Swiss is a daring adventurer in a mediocre society, and his presence gives the film comic overtones. No equivalent character exists in *Le Mariage*; here there is only desolation.

However, Lelouch does not go as far as he might have in analyzing the couple. The four-segment plot, the autonomy given to Rufus and Ogier, and the yellow tint are all distancing devices that limit the involvement of author and spectator in the film. Instead of getting at why the marriage has disintegrated, the film mainly shows us symptoms: hatred, screaming, an unlivable environment, a child estranged from his father. The distancing devices may provide a way for Lelouch to deal with subject matter that is difficult, sensitive, and alien to his usual concerns. For example, the freedom given to Rufus to improvise his role results in a ranting and raving character who is far more negative than anyone else in Lelouch's work. But the film loses a great deal by remaining an exterior view of the characters. It gives a scattered, impressionistic picture of a failed marriage rather than getting right to the heart of the matter. So, although *Le Mariage* is a fascinating film, it remains a sketch, an experiment.

Cat and Mouse (*Le Chat et la souris*, 1975)

M. Richard (Jean-Pierre Aumont), one of the richest men in France, is killed in mysterious circumstances at his home outside Paris. Several extremely valuable paintings are stolen from his home at the same time. Inspector Lechat (Serge Reggiani) and his assistant (Philippe Léotard) appear on the scene to investigate the crime. Mme. Richard (Michèle Morgan) is the leading suspect, even though she was supposedly watching a film on the Champs Elysées when the death occurred. Lechat feels that Mme. Richard is guilty, and spends considerable energy trying to pierce her alibi. An insurance adjustor withholds payment on the loss of the paintings based on the inspector's suspicions. However, Lechat is removed from the case and actually retired early from the police by the minister of the interior. The new detective in charge of the case is told that M. Richard's death was part of a leftist plot.

Lechat retires to a farmhouse in Normandy, but he continues to investigate the Richard case for a book he is writing. He eventually discovers how Mme. Richard could have killed her husband and returned to the Champs Elysées within two hours. Confronted with this evidence, she simply laughs, and Lechat concludes that she is innocent. Investigating further, he finds the insurance agent and the Richards' ex-servants involved in various crimes. There was no murder, though; M. Richard had killed himself.

Lelouch has made strangely deprecating comments about *Cat and Mouse* to the press. For example, he told Christine Gauthey of *Le Journal du Dimanche* that the film was an expedient, a way to recover from the disastrous *And Now My Love* and the noncommercial *Le Mariage:* "I wrote a diverting police story, trying to make it as dignified as possible; funny, but never hitting below the belt. This is a genre which I know how to do, and which has saved me several times. *The Crook, Happy New Year,* and *Cat and Mouse* are to some extent my trilogy of good luck. There's no risk. I could make only this kind of film, but I want to do other things."[3]

Despite the director's comments, there are advantages to working with familiar material. Lelouch tells the story effortlessly and with great style. His direction is clean, crisp, and funny, with a touch of bravado. Nuances of character behavior are often more important than the dialogue of a scene. The film makes very good use of subjective camera shots, which personalize Lechat's work; a murder investigation becomes

Cat and Mouse—Philippe Léotard, Serge Reggiani, and Sam, the half-trained police dog. (Quartet Films)

a series of impressions and personal interactions. Lelouch also uses many other surprises, complications, and stylistic flourishes. For example, the film includes several different kinds of flashbacks: two versions of the same scene, biased flashbacks, shock cuts to the past, totally imagined scenes.

The plot of *Cat and Mouse* may be only a pretext for Lelouch's observations and digressions. The question of who shot M. Richard is never particularly gripping. Instead, the film explores characters and setting and creates a mood. The characters live in a comfortable, middle-class world typified by the high-rise suburbs west of Paris, where M. Richard builds skyscrapers and Lechat resides in a modern apartment. Unlike the heroes of *A Man and a Woman* or *Life, Love, Death*, however, these characters are not lonely or confused or obsessed in a modern setting. In fact, they take tremendous pleasure in their lives. Lechat, our protagonist, enjoys his work but also takes time to eat well, talk well, train his police dog, and spend a few hours with his mistress. A tremendous amount of time is spent at the table: eating has always represented a kind of harmony with life in Lelouch's films, and in *Cat and Mouse* this harmony is ever present. We should also note that the "cat" and "mouse" of the title are Lechat ("the cat," in French) and Mme. Richard, so that the police investigation becomes a way to meet and court a desirable woman. At the end of the film, Lechat and Mme. Richard are clearly about to have an affair.

A few key scenes illustrate the film's warm, happy mood. The opening sequence features the camera in a slowly ascending construction elevator looking out on a gorgeous view of Paris. When the ascent stops, we cut to M. Richard, inside the elevator, who utters the film's first word: "Alors?" A moment later, Mme. Richard pushes her husband into the void; he falls with a lyrical, graceful motion. Then the scene is repeated, and we see that Mme. Richard only daydreamed about pushing her husband. She describes her fantasy, and Richard's comment is, "Do you love me that much?" This scene beautifully sets up the rest of the film. The informal dialogue reintroduces the warm, relaxed tone that is characteristic of Lelouch (but absent from *Le Mariage*), and the false murder sets up the complications and hidden motives of the mystery plot. Further, the opening scene is a paradigm for the entire film: a tragedy, the death of M. Richard, only momentarily interrupts an idyllic existence.

Andrew Sarris, a fine critic who seems to be a bit ashamed of enjoying Lelouch's movies, says that the false murder "marks Lelouch as a lightweight in the medium."[4] His comment is evidently based on an idea of authorial integrity; an author or director may provide false clues, but he should not so blatantly manipulate the spectator's expectations. Sarris's position overlooks two things: first, the imagined murder is convincingly motivated by Mme. Richard's attitude toward her husband; and second, *Cat and Mouse* is not really a classic mystery (where authorial integrity would be an important concept), but rather a comic film based on mystery elements. Thus, the splendid opening is thoroughly justified.

Another extraordinary scene has Léotard, the assistant, coming to have dinner with Lechat and his daughter (whom the assistant has not previously met). Léotard gets lost in the look-alike buildings of a huge apartment development and arrives very late.[5] Lechat's daughter is not impressed, and Léotard's feeble attempts to ingratiate himself fall flat. Suddenly, though, all three characters burst out laughing at the incongruity of the situation. An uncomfortable scene becomes a warm family gathering, and the two young people are married soon afterwards. The dinner scene is perhaps the best expression of the film's joie de vivre.

Excellent acting and casting add to the pleasures of *Cat and Mouse*. Reggiani combines the strength of an action hero with the charm and urbanity of an entertainer (he is, in fact, both actor and singer). Sympathetic, relaxed, aging a little but still marvelously alert, he is perfectly

Cat and Mouse—Michèle Morgan and Philippe Léotard. (Quartet Films)

cast as a worldly policeman who is rarely surprised but often amused by human conduct. More generally, the use of such mature actors (Morgan was born in 1920, Reggiani in 1922) suggests that the film's emphasis on simple pleasures is based on long experience. The casting of Morgan was a great publicity coup for Lelouch; once the grand lady of the French screen, she had been retired for eight years before appearing in *Cat and Mouse*. One of the film's incidental charms is watching the once commanding Morgan in a light role. However, she often seems a bit distracted as the attractive but putupon middle-aged lady. Not until the very end of the film, when she begins to respond to Reggiani, do her warmth and sparkle as an actress come through.

The supporting roles include such memorable types as the charmingly crooked insurance agent, the polite but opportunistic servants, and the hard-headed porno star who is M. Richard's mistress. Jean-Pierre Aumont gives a quiet, dignified performance as M. Richard, and Philippe Léotard is amusing as Reggiani's assistant. Lelouch has come a long way from a film like *Live for Life*, where the supporting characters are empty shells. Here he creates a vivid rogues' gallery around the two protagonists.

The disturbing aspect of all this pleasure is the cynicism needed to achieve it. Lechat is corrupt, as are most of the characters in the film. Lechat supplements his income by taking occasional payoffs from crooks, he gets special treatment for his prostitute-mistress, and he derives various other privileges from his position and knowledge. His superiors know that he cheats; in one scene the minister says, "Lechat touche" (Lechat is on the take) and a subordinate replies, "Better a policeman on the take who makes arrests than an honest policeman who doesn't." The excuse for Lechat's conduct seems to be that he owes no allegiance to a bankrupt institution like the government, which cynically manipulates M. Richard's death for its own political ends. At least Lechat is independent; as he tells Mme. Richard, he was "never really *with* the police—at least, not profoundly." Also, Lechat's private investigation of the Richard case probably involves a sense of justice as well as curiosity and the attraction of Mme. Richard.

Still, Lechat is not much different from the minister, or from the insurance agent who doubles as fence-kidnapper-robber. Not even Mme. Richard is completely pure; she has an affair with her son's best friend (her son died in an auto crash) and then declares, "I'm ashamed." This brief scene is particularly interesting because Mme. Richard had just told Lechat that her relationship with the young man was entirely platonic. She has misled Lechat and, perhaps, herself. Mme. Richard has not committed any crimes, but the film makes a point of showing that she is not completely removed from the surrounding duplicity and corruption.

Since right and wrong are so relative, one cannot get too excited about government corruption. The film appears to be an exposé but is actually quite complacent about corruption in high places. So, Lechat's reaction to the Richard cover-up is to investigate for a book. He wants to understand the government's manipulations and even to profit from them; he has no great desire to change anything. Following a similar logic, Lechat does not turn in the various crooks. He repairs injustice himself by demanding that the insurance man and the servants repay Mme. Richard.

Lelouch comments: "Policemen who protect call girls, earn money on the side, these things exist. Why not show them? I'm only communicating a fact which is more or less officially admitted. . . . Before, the censors wouldn't have let me do it. Now it's abolished and a minister came to see the premiere and really liked it."[6] Lelouch thus places himself in the long French tradition of moral realism. However, his vision of how people really live has a flaw: it is too simple, too easy, too flat. Corruption of all kinds is taken very lightly. None of the selfish individualists in the film causes any permanent harm, so questions of responsibility are avoided. The only one hurt is M. Richard, who wanted to die. Corruption leads to an increase in pleasure, and the characters live happily ever after in an amoral world.

Cat and Mouse bears an interesting relationship to Agnès Varda's Le Bonheur (1965). In that film, which was lushly photographed in a rural, pastoral France, a young woman kills herself after her husband candidly admits he is doubling his pleasure with another woman. Instead of feeling any guilt, the husband simply marries his mistress, and he and his family (including two small kids) live happily ever after. The perfect beauty and harmony of the film is a stylization, a distancing device. Varda uses it to strikingly pose questions of responsibility, conflicting values, hedonism, and the like. Cat and Mouse presents a similar, though perhaps more restrained, vision of amoral happiness. But for Lelouch, this vision is not a stylization; he seems to be serious. In Cat and Mouse moral relativism causes no passions, no conflicts, no difficulties. We are left with that sugarcoated world view which Varda satirizes so well.

The Good and the Bad (Le Bon et les méchants, 1976)

The commercial success of Cat and Mouse restored Lelouch's reputation as a popular filmmaker and encouraged him to take on a more ambitious project. He had been working on a film about gangsters under the German Occupation at least since 1970, when he researched French gangsterism for The Crook. At that time he encountered the book Tu trahiras sans vergogne (You Will Betray without Shame) by Philippe Aziz, a sensationalized account of the careers of petty crook Henri Lafont and ex-police officer Pierre Bonny, who established their own little empire in the Paris Gestapo.[7] In 1970 Lelouch talked abut making a film about Bonny and Lafont, "an enormous history of gangsterism, as terrifying as The Godfather, as bloody and as unbelievable . . . A Chicago-like atmosphere, but with political resonances that are even more terrible."[8]

When Lelouch shot this extraordinary subject in 1975 as The Good and the Bad, the focus had changed considerably. The sinister Bonny and Lafont were now only background figures, and, though terrifying in spots, the film was in many respects a comedy. Still, the basic theme of gangsters exploiting the Occupation remained.

The film begins in 1935. Blond, handsome Jacques (Jacques Dutronc) and squat, homely Simon (Jacques Villeret) are auto mechanics who dream of better things. Jacques first tries a career as a boxer, but gives up when he is knocked out by future champion Marcel Cerdan. Jacques and Simon then turn to crime, ignoring an offer from gang leader Henri Lafont to rob post offices and banks on their own. They steal a new Citroën with front-wheel drive to make getaways, and thus earn the name "Le gang des tractions avant" ("The Front-Wheel-Drive Gang"). Lola (Marlène Jobert), whom Jacques meets in a dance hall, becomes the third member of the gang.

The crooks' first robbery brings them to the attention of Inspector Bruno Deschamps (Bruno Cremer), a police official who has married the boss's daughter, Dominique (Brigitte Fossey), to advance his career. Deschamps is their main adversary throughout the next ten years. Further, in the style of *And Now My Love*, the lives of the five major characters are intertwined throughout the film, even though Jacques and Bruno never meet. Family dinner is juxtaposed with family dinner, and the formal wedding of Bruno contrasts vividly with the raucous and unofficial "marriage" of Jacques and Lola.

World War II and the Occupation of France are shown only by a shot of schoolchildren learning German, with a picture of Marshal Pétain on the wall. Then we see Bruno, who was called to Vichy, deciding to work for the Pétain government and the Germans, despite Dominique's objections. The gang faces a similar decision when caught on a train (because Simon, a Jew, has been circumcised); they demand to be taken to their friend Lafont in Paris. Invited to joint Lafont's gangsters in robbing Jews, they instead hijack a shipment of stolen paintings bound for Germany. This creates a whole chain of complications: the Germans blame the Resistance and take hostages; Simon returns the paintings; two other gangsters involved in the hijacking squeal to the police; Lola is arrested and tortured; the two disloyal gangsters are killed in a booby-trapped car.

Already exciting, the film gets very intense when Jacques telephones Gestapo headquarters with the message: "You kidnapped my wife, I kidnapped yours. If you kill my wife, I'll kill yours." The two wives are exchanged, Lola half dead for Dominique unharmed. After this Jacques and the gang join the Resistance because they "have a score to settle with the Hitler gang." Dominique, always hostile to the Germans, seeks out Jacques and passes him secret information for the Resistance; they also have a love affair. When Dominique is caught, she blames her husband, and, in another astonishing scene, Deschamps is told to shoot either himself or his wife, whoever is guilty. He shoots Dominique, but is sent to prison anyway. Meanwhile, Jacques is arrested as he comes to meet Dominique, and is sent to the same prison.

The film indicates the war's end with another shot of the schoolroom, where the children are now learning English. Then we see General de Gaulle decorating a line of Resistants, including both Jacques and Deschamps. Celebrating later in a bistro, Lola asks Jacques if, now that he is a hero, he will get a real job. But in the next scene, Jacques steals another Citroën, and Deschamps, now assistant prefect of police, gets a call about the Front-Wheel-Drive Gang. The film ends with a title: "The story of the Front-Wheel-Drive Gang really begins here. Maybe one day we'll tell it to you. . . ."

Lelouch says that everything that happens in the film is true, although he has "simplified" things by "centering all these events on five or six characters."[9] His claim appears overstated, for although the Front-Wheel-Drive Gang, Lafont, Bonny, and, presumably, Deschamps are based on real people, the film drastically alters history. For example, Lafont was not a dashing gangster but a miserable petty crook before the war, and the character of Jacques seems completely unrelated to Armand le Fou, the leader of the Front-Wheel-Drive Gang described by Aziz.[10] Lelouch has used fact as merely the starting point for fiction.

The Good and the Bad draws at least as much from other films as it does from history. It is clearly Lelouch's contribution to "la mode rétro," a large and distinguished group of recent European films set in the 1930s and 1940s. Like *Stavisky, The Garden of the Finzi-Continis, The Conformist*, and many others, Lelouch's film combines a romantic-nostalgic view of the period with political moralizing.* More specifically, Lelouch's film follows *The Sorrow and the Pity* (Marcel Ophuls, 1971) and *Lacombe, Lucien* (Louis Malle, 1974) as a reevaluation of the German Occupation of France. All three films puncture the myth of a country dominated by the Resistance to show various kinds of French collaboration with the Nazis.

The Good and the Bad also shows the influence of *Bonnie and Clyde* (Arthur Penn, 1967) and other American movies. The Front-Wheel-Drive Gang corresponds very closely to the Parker-Barrow gang in Arthur Penn's film: Jacques Dutronc plays the handsome, daring Warren Beatty role, Marlène Jobert plays the willowy Faye Dunaway role, and Jacques Villeret plays the chubby sidekick à la Michael J. Pollard. Both films present the gangs as romantic, sympathetic rebels, and both feature casual but elegant period costumes. Even the importance of automobiles in Lelouch's film echoes *Bonnie and Clyde*. One can also see the influence of American "buddy" movies *(The Sting, Butch Cassidy and the Sundance Kid)* on Lelouch's film in the importance of the male-male friendship and the mixture of light, almost slapstick comedy with violent action.

Even closer than the American connection is the link between *The*

---

*The nostalgic treatment in *The Good and the Bad* is strongly reinforced by the use of sepia photography throughout. The film is not exactly black-and-white, but rather various shades of brown.

Good and the Bad and *And Now My Love*. The story spread out over ten years, the interplay between history and personal life, the interlocking of five characters, the superbly composed sequence shots, and the emphasis on music all connect *The Good and the Bad* to the earlier film. However, Lelouch has worked out some of *And Now My Love*'s rough spots. Here the brief, vivid, impressionistic scenes are linked to a strong story line, and the characters' motivations are firmly rooted in the wartime experience. With this foundation, the actors give uniformly fine performances. Jacques Dutronc, a pop star turned actor, is particularly impressive as a low-keyed man of action.

Musically, this film approaches the high standard set by *And Now My Love*. Francis Lai's score presents various aspects of the war, from the strident optimism of a German march to badly played classical music at Vichy to the contraband delights of American jazz. Big-band jazz and dance music dominate the sound track, representing the intangible freedoms the gang is fighting for. As Lola says about jazz, "The Americans will win the war because the Germans can't make music like that." In one lovely scene, Simon puts on a contraband American record to cheer up the convalescing Lola, and in midtune the amplification swells up to show a renewal of hope. The music is both objectively present and subjectively experienced by the characters.

Morality, an implicit issue in many of Lelouch's films, is explicitly the subject here. Who is good and who is bad? Following Ophuls and Malle, Lelouch shows the German Occupation of France as a period of extreme moral ambiguity. Though Jacques's band joins the Resistance and Inspector Deschamps assists the Gestapo, the motives and morals of both sides are complex. Lelouch insists on this point with an opening title: "There are no profoundly good or bad men, there are only men of good or bad humor." Thus, morality is relative, and largely a product of circumstance, as in *Cat and Mouse*.

However, despite this title, which seems to have been an afterthought,[11] morality in *The Good and the Bad* involves something more than opportunism or circumstance. This can best be demonstrated by following the series of choices made by the characters. The Front-Wheel-Drive Gang's first difficult choice takes place in Lafont's headquarters, where the gang is offered Gestapo protection. Jacques seems tempted by the opportunity of pillaging Jews for the Nazis, but Simon and Lola huddle together defensively amidst the militarism, pomp, and decadence of Lafont's surroundings. Their negative reaction evidently wins the day, for the gang reasserts its independence by stealing from the Germans.

The next decision is forced by the German army's taking hostages, shown brutally in one long take of troops entering a church on Sunday and removing all of the adult men. Will the gang return the stolen paintings, or will it sacrifice the hostages for private gain? Jacques complains bitterly about being confused with the Resistance. "I am not a Resistant," he says, "I'm a small-time crook [un petit voyou]." Still, Simon and Lola convince him that the paintings should be returned. Lelouch cleverly indicates another possible choice through the feud with the other accomplices. These two characters barely have speaking roles, but they are nicely type-cast. Their glowering faces alone suggest that such hardened professional gangsters would not be influenced by moral niceties.

Lelouch also shows us options in Deschamps' decision-making. At Vichy, Deschamps says that it is only natural for a French civil servant to work for the Vichy government, but Dominique points out that he will really be working for the Germans. She urges him to join de Gaulle in London. Later, in the scene of Dominique's murder, Lelouch visually presents an unspoken alternative. Deschamps is supposed to kill Dominique or himself, but as he picks up the pistol, the Gestapo commander's belly fills a substantial part of the frame. He could have turned on this officer; instead he shoots Dominique.

After Lola is tortured and released, Jacques and Simon join the Resistance. The film does not clearly explain why they do this. Jacques, Simon, and Lola made the earlier moral decisions following a very basic idea of fair play and an instinctive reaction against the Germans. Joining the Resistance could be a logical extension of these feelings, especially since the episode of the paintings shows the Germans interfering with the gang's freedom of action. However, when questioned by a Resistance leader (Serge Reggiani), Jacques gives another motive for joining the Resistance. "I have a score to settle with the Hitler gang," he says. So, Jacques makes a political decision for purposes of personal revenge.

Lelouch has supported both possible motives in interviews. In an interview in *France-Soir*, he said, "For me, someone who's good is simple and direct. Someone who's bad is complicated." Lelouch described the Dutronc character as "an instinctive person who goes straight to the heart of every problem."[12] This suggests that Jacques, the simple one, instinctively chooses the right side of the conflict, whereas the more complicated Deschamps makes the wrong choice. However, when I asked Lelouch why Jacques joined the Resistance, he responded that it was "uniquely for personal reasons . . . to take revenge for the evil done to his wife."[13]

So, are there such things as good and bad, or not? Lelouch refuses to rule out that Jacques, the hero, is simply a petty gangster who joins the Resistance by accident. Similarly, Deschamps is not necessarily a "méchant"; he may only be an opportunist. However, the whole melodramatic structure of the film moves toward making Jacques "good" and Deschamps "bad." Jacques is a daring, independent, and instinctive

underdog; by contrast, Deschamps is an ambitious, glib, and unprin-
cipled government official. This dichotomy culminates in the marvelous
scene in which Jaques and Deschamps are decorated after the war. The
scene is *not* a demonstration of moral relativism because the audience
cannot contain its displeasure and feels compelled to boo and hiss Deschamps.

Ultimately, the film seems not only ambiguous but also a bit incoherent because the moral issues are never resolved. It creates an emotional
distinction between good and bad that is not backed up intellectually.
This may be quite realistic, since people caught up in a melodramatic
situation are not necessarily "profoundly good or bad." In Lelouch's film
we see both the black-and-white of melodrama and the gray area of
character motivation. Still, the lack of resolution is uncomfortable.
Lelouch cheats the spectator, in a certain sense, by not making up his
mind about good and bad.

The general tone of *The Good and the Bad* also presents problems. Is
it possible to make a comedy about the German Occupation? Does the
film's nostalgic, sentimental approach do justice to the subject? Would
the tragic dimensions of *M. Klein* (Joseph Losey, 1976) or the calm
seriousness of *Les Violins du bal* (Michel Drach, 1973) be more fitting?

The key question is whether the comic and sentimental aspects of
Lelouch's film aid or conflict with the reevaluation of the Occupation.
The Good and the Bad emulates, to a great extent, Malle's *Lacombe,
Lucien,* which has many light moments and maintains a degree of sympathy for the main character. Lucien Lacombe is an unsophisticated
teenager who joins the French Gestapo without fully understanding the
consequences of his act. However, Malle's film retains an underlying
sense of the brutality and horror of the Gestapo. The film ends with a
title announcing that Lucien was executed by the Resistance.

The Good and the Bad tries to expand on Malle's subtle view of the
period, but the tone is so light and the characters so sympathetic that an
underlying sense of justice and morality is sometimes difficult to grasp.
Jacques and Simon wisecrack and improvise their way through various
situations, so that we often seem to be watching a high-spirited adventure that happens to be set in the 1940s. The mood does change,
though, as life-or-death decisions are required in the film's second half.
Moments like the taking of French hostages, the double kidnapping,
and the shooting of Dominique are treated seriously (although a comic
interlude interrupts the kidnapping, and the extreme simplicity of the
shooting scene is Grand Guignolesque). As in *And Now My Love*,
Lelouch's point is that people generally live in the private world represented by the comic scenes, and only occasionally confront history.
However, by presenting much of the Occupation as a comic adventure,
the film risks trivializing it.

MARLENE JOBERT · JACQUES DUTRONC
BRUNO CREMER · BRIGITTE FOSSEY
JACQUES VILLERET
dans

un film de
CLAUDE
LELOUCH

VASSILIEV

LE BON
ET LES MECHANTS

JEAN-PIERRE KALFON avec la participation de SERGE REGGIANI

musique de FRANCIS LAI

Poster for *The Good and the Bad*. Note that the romantic couple dominates, while the swastika in the Arc de Triomphe (the only indication of a political or historical theme) is quite small. (Private collection)

Almost lost in the tangle of issues surrounding this film is an extraordinary portrait of male-female relationships. Both female characters are active, capable people who deal with men as equals. Lola is a full member of the gang, and Dominique breaks with her collaborator husband to work for the Resistance. The women are actually stronger and more acute morally than the men; even Jacques has to be convinced not to join with Lafont. Lelouch also shows that the exclusive couple is not the only possible relationship. Simon and Lola are simply friends, and the affair of Dominique and Jacques is part politics and part infatuation. The most interesting moment in the film's picture of relationships comes in the final scene. Lola, dancing with Jacques, asks him in a chiding yet affectionate way if he loved Dominique. A little bit, he says, a very little bit, and they keep on dancing. Affection, sadness, acceptance, honesty, reserve, humor, and optimism all mingle in this brief moment. It shows how far Lelouch has progressed in his direction of actors, and indeed, in his understanding of men and women.

The best critique of *The Good and the Bad* comes from Henri Béhar, who reports on two viewings of the film. On the first viewing, Béhar questions the propriety of a comedy about the Occupation but seems impressed by the film. He especially praises the acting of Fossey, Villeret, Jobert, and Dutronc. On his second viewing, he finds the film "dangerous," saying that "its charm leads you to accept . . . a certain number of inadmissible propositions." For example, the film suggests that "the war was only a parenthesis between two slow dances."[14] Both reviews are correct, and they define some of the film's complexity. *The Good and the Bad* is an incredibly charming and well-made film, but its ideas are confused, and perhaps even dangerous. Despite the obvious care that Lelouch has taken in sketching out moral choices, the film's ambiguity and its lightness of tone may gloss over the serious issues raised by the Occupation period.

The Good and the Bad was a big commercial success in France, and played very briefly in the United States. Unfortunately, this fascinating and potentially controversial film has been almost completely ignored by critics outside the French daily papers. It will probably be rediscovered and marveled at some day.

Si c'était à refaire (A Second Chance, 1976)

The opening shot shows Catherine Berger (Catherine Deneuve) being released from prison. She walks down corridors, retrieves her belongings, and emerges into the outside world in one four-minute take. The prison is clean and modern and its staff is sympathetic, but still prison is a metaphor for constraint and unfreedom, here as in other Lelouch films. Thus, this film is about Catherine's rebirth.

Catherine goes to Aix-en-Provence to see her son, who thinks he is a parentless orphan, at boarding school. Back in Paris, she applies for a secretarial job. At this point the film flashes back fifteen years to another job and the circumstances that landed her in jail. Twenty-year-old Catherine works in a bank. The bank president gets her to work late one evening and rapes her. Catherine and her fiancé, Henri, stop the bank president on a deserted road; Henri beats him and accidentally kills him. Both Henri and Catherine are convicted of murder, and Henri kills himself in prison.

Catherine, imprisoned and in need of something to live for, decides to have a baby. Her lawyer (Charles Denner) refuses to impregnate her, so she seduces a rather stupid attendant at the prison hospital. Her scheme succeeds: she gives birth to a boy, who is raised under her lawyer's supervision.

The exposition now completed, the film returns to its main action. Catherine and Lucienne (mother of the dead Henri, played by Colette Baudot) take Simon (Catherine's son, played by Jean-Jacques Briot) with them for a vacation at the beach. Catherine thrives in the warm, sensual atmosphere with her new family unit. She spoils Simon with presents. Simon likes the attention, but misinterprets it; he writes a friend that he is going to score with the pretty, older blonde. Catherine encourages Simon's interest in a girl his own age, but he prefers flirting with his mother. Finally, she reveals their relationship, and the idyll at the beach continues.

In Paris, Catherine gets an apartment with Simon and Lucienne. She finds a low-pressure job at a lamp store owned by Monsieur Alexandre (Alexandre Mnouchkine). One day Sarah Gordon (Anouk Aimée), a compulsive thief and Catherine's former cell-mate, comes to the apartment and joins the ménage. Sarah also finds work at the lamp shop.

In an extraordinary scene, Catherine comes into the glass-enclosed lamp store, locks the door, and confronts Sarah. "How could you?" she says. "So you know," Sarah responds. We assume that Sarah has been stealing from Monsieur Alexandre, but something quite different is going on. Catherine is upset because Sarah has seduced fifteen-year-old Simon. Sarah protests that Catherine is angry only because her best friend was the one who did it. Catherine agrees with her but remains angry.

Simon insists on taking Catherine and Sarah to a bloody boxing match. The match is an excuse for him to introduce Catherine to Patrick (Francis Huster), Simon's charismatic history teacher, whom they run into at intermission. Simon pulls Sarah away, leaving Patrick and Catherine to chat at the bar. Naturally, they like each other.

Si c'était à refaire—Catherine Deneuve and Anouk Aimée on Mont Blanc. (The Museum of Modern Art/Film Stills Archive)

The film ends with Catherine, Sarah, Simon, and Patrick climbing Mont Blanc (boxing and climbing are Patrick's obsessions). Camped on the mountain, Catherine tells Patrick her life story—thus explaining, retroactively, the voice-over narration that accompanies the movie. The next day, a shot from a helicopter shows four small figures on Mont Blanc. The figures hug each other, and the helicopter ascends into the sky. Snow is a symbol of rebirth here, as it was in *Live for Life*.

Si c'était à refaire is clearly Lelouch's film about feminism, expanding the picture of the independent woman he had started in *Happy New Year*. The publicity release for *Si c'était à refaire* describes the film as "a return to life in a society where the condition of women has made a jump of several centuries in fifteen years."[15] Lelouch presents women who earn their own living and structure their own lives. Conventional family arrangements are replaced by new groupings; Catherine lives first with Simon and Lucienne, who could have been Simon's grandmother but is not, and then with Simon and Sarah. This reflects both Catherine's reluctance to deal with men and new support systems among women. Sexual customs are reevaluated; is there anything drastically wrong with a boy of fifteen sleeping with a woman of forty? Strong friendships between women become important; Lelouch notes that the bond between Catherine and Sarah is analogous to the friendships between males that are so common in movies of the last ten years.[16]

The film's melodramatic emphasis clashes with its interesting view of feminism. To begin with, the "crime film" flashback is not too exciting in itself, and it gives a false sense of how the film will develop. If the main function of the flashback and related scenes is to turn Catherine into Rip Van Winkle, why is the exposition made so elaborate? This is one of Lelouch's less successful excursions in changing the tone of a narrative. Other melodramatic and sentimental elements are also irritating. The character of Patrick, for example, is stereotyped as Prince Charming and the symbolism of Mont Blanc is too blatant. Worst of all, the film is accompanied by an insipidly cheerful Francis Lai melody that suggests that Catherine's problems are solved almost from the outset.

The central character of Catherine has itself been laced with sentimentality. Except for a hesitation about dealing with men, she has evidently been untouched by her experiences. She is simple, healthy, wholesome, and immaculately dressed—in many ways the ideal housewife. She has a surprising passivity for a self-reliant woman. As played by Catherine Deneuve, the character is as much a princess waiting to wake up as a woman creating her own destiny. Of course, Miss Deneuve has always been beautiful but passive on film.

At least Deneuve has the sunny disposition and sensuality to bring off Catherine's reawakening at the beach. On vacation, she unwinds, suns, eats, laughs, and goes to a dance. Her appetites return, and with them a

sense of normalcy. Sensuality also requires a resolution of the relationship with Simon. A key scene here shows Catherine and Simon dancing
to music from a cassette recorder. Simon does not know he is dancing
with his mother, whereas Catherine's behavior is very ambiguous. She
is having innocent fun with Simon, but she is also trying out her emotions on a "safe" man and expressing an Oedipal need for her long-lost
son. This complex situation pushes Catherine to explain herself to Simon, and thus make a further return to normalcy.

If Catherine Deneuve's acting is only partly successful, Anouk Aimée
is a delight. Tall, lean, and casually dressed, with short hair and a few
facial wrinkles, she is very much the independent woman not looking for
a man but not exactly not looking, either. Her mystery and grace, so
apparent in *A Man and a Woman,* are now joined by experience, intelligence, and good humor. Her character is a person of consequence and a
good friend, the female equivalent of Lino Ventura or Charles Gérard in
Happy New Year. She steals many scenes with her half-bantering but
basically serious conversation. Aimée had not acted in films for seven
years before *Si c'était à refaire,* so her casting was in itself a triumph for
Lelouch. After the film, she returned to her role in private life as the
wife of British actor Albert Finney.

The friendship of Catherine and Sarah, as equal to equal, works very
well. The sensuous, passive Catherine is complemented by the more
active, more sardonic Sarah. Even more important, the two actresses
seem to give each other a lift. The film gets livelier and more amusing
when both are on the screen together, so that we can actually see the
benefits of their friendship. Lelouch comments: "One cannot make a
film about friendship unless the people being filmed feel involved. For-
tunately, real bonds of friendship unite Catherine and Anouk."[17]

Both actresses help make the scene in the lamp shop a tour de force.
Aimée is wonderful as someone who has been caught breaking conventional morality, but who sees good reason not to repent. Her soothing
explanations are tinged by guilt. Deneuve is almost as good as an over-
protective and conservative parent who can still see Aimée's point of
view. The scene also gains a great deal from Lelouch's directing technique. He presents it in one long take, letting the relationship develop
in real time and space. The beauty of the actresses and of their surroundings tones down the argument. Slight changes of camera position
reflect subtleties of interaction. As a final touch, Lelouch keeps shooting
after completing the scene as written, leaving the actors to improvise
with some guidance from behind the camera.[18] This results in a conversation, informal to begin with, which becomes more disorganized and
high-spirited as it goes on. In the disorder, Catherine's anger is dis-
solved by friendship.

The ultimate problem with *Si c'était à refaire* is that it has far too much plot. Lelouch's observations of new women and changing mores are very good. Why, then, does he need such an old-fashioned potboiler of a plot? A simpler, looser structure on the model of *One Sings, the Other Doesn't* (Agnès Varda, 1977) or *Jules and Jim* (François Truffaut, 1963), or even *Un homme qui me plaît* would have been more effective. Lelouch has certainly mastered the plotting of adventure films, but he stumbles when he tries to make a woman's picture.

Another Man, Another Chance (1977)

In 1977, James Caan is an advertising photographer hired to shoot a "Western" tableau involving four Belgian show horses hitched to a Cadillac, with three models in old-fashioned dresses sitting on the car. He objects that the scene has nothing to do with the West, adding that he has photographs taken by his great-grandmother which show what the West was really like.

After this prologue, the film cuts between two parallel stories. The first begins in Paris under siege by the Prussian army in the winter of 1870–71. Francis (Francis Huster) meets Jeanne (Genevieve Bujold) while photographing the breadline outside her father's bakery. Jeanne visits his photography studio for a wedding picture; she is engaged to an army officer. Then she calls off the wedding at a family dinner and arrives at Francis's doorstep at 6:00 A.M. They decide to go to America.

Meanwhile, in a small Western town, David Williams (James Caan), a veterinarian, is quarreling with his wife Mary (Jennifer Warren). She complains that he spends too much time working, drinking, and gambling. After the birth of their son, Simon, Mary wants to return to Philadelphia, but David refuses. One day, while David is playing billiards on horseback, three bandits rape and murder his wife. David takes Simon to boarding school and sets up a new practice in Roll Point, Texas.

Francis and Jeanne travel from New York to the West and set up a photography business in nearby Redland, Texas. The imaginative Francis starts working for a newspaper. A flashback late in the film shows Francis's death. He refuses to give up the picture he took of a hanging, so the hanged man's father shoots him. Jeanne bears a child, Sarah, and continues the photography business.

Following an unobtrusive ellipse of a few years, David and Jeanne meet at Alice's boarding school, where both have come to see their children. David drives her home in his buckboard. The next Sunday they take their children on a picnic and get along well. However, Jeanne tells David that she will not see him again; she is still in love with her husband.

David enters a handicap race for horses, buckboards, and runners sponsored by the local newspaper (a promotional idea that had been suggested years before by Francis). Riding his superb horse Durango, David finishes second to an Indian runner. Jeanne sends him her "casquette" (cap) by stagecoach to show him that she cares for him. But David is not at his hotel; he has been summoned to provide medical care for the same outlaws who killed Mary (identified by an Indian good luck charm that she wore). He kills them all, returns to town, and rides off immediately to find Jeanne. He finds her picnicking with the kids near the boarding school. The four of them run together and the film freezes to sepia, evidently indicating one of the photographs that James Caan, in 1977, said would show "the real West."*

Lelouch describes the film's plot like this: "There are people who advance, people who will meet each other, one more time, as in all my films, people who, without knowing it, advance toward each other. These people will encounter the most terrible moments of their lives, without knowing that these terrible moments announce their happiest moments."[19] Jeanne and Francis cross an ocean and endure the hardships of a wagon train to start again in a new land. David makes a new start after Mary's death. The opening bars of Beethoven's Fifth Symphony (the dominant musical motif of the film's first half) underline the gravity and fatefulness of their situations. The film's long-take, moving camera style adds a connotation of journeying, moving toward some distant goal.

The juxtaposition of the stories of people who have not yet met is, of course, borrowed from *And Now My Love*. As in the earlier film, the main characters in this film are bound together by various correspondences and coincidences. Their love at the end will "solve" the film's narrative and give emotional depth and meaning to what has gone before.

The film connects even more explicitly to Lelouch's first big success, *A Man and a Woman*. The situation of a widow and a widower, each with a child, who meet and start a new life together is an exact repeat of the earlier film. For *Another Man, Another Chance* (during production it was called *Another Man, Another Woman*), Lelouch has changed the setting and eliminated most of the flashbacks. For much of the film we see no correspondence with its predecessor, but when David meets Jeanne at the boarding school and drives her home, the scene is a startlingly exact replica of Jean-Louis and Anne meeting in *A Man and a Woman*. Caan's buckboard replaces Trintignant's Ford Mustang. After this, parallels proliferate and the films end at the same point—the

*Since all four characters are in the picture, Jeanne must have set her camera for a delayed exposure before David appeared. Still, it is extremely unlikely that this photograph could have been made in the scene Lelouch shows us.

woman rejects the man, then the characters meet again and demonstrate their love. The point of Lelouch's quote from himself is evidently that some stories are so basic that they transcend time and space.

Historically, the film turns on bringing together two realities, American and European, which are almost always considered separately. In France, 1870–71 is the period of the Franco-Prussian War, the fall of Napoleon III, and the Commune of Paris. In the United States, 1870 marks the height of westward migration after the Civil War. It is precisely the period of the Western film. Lelouch juxtaposes the two realities by presenting someone between cultures. As he says, "The film is the story of a European state of mind" that, "in two generations, becomes American."[20] This theme allows the director to say something about France, America, and the relationship between the two. Lelouch adds that the film has a contemporary significance: "I think that there are a lot of Europeans who would like to leave Europe, but who don't have a taste for adventure."[21] As always, he advocates taking the risk.

The scenes of Paris are not at all analytical; they simply show that things are very bad in Europe. Lelouch comments: "Eating rats, eating dogs, eating cats, people killing each other, hunger was so bad during the siege of Paris that they even ate people."[22] Lelouch avoids any discussion of the political situation that caused this mess. The Paris Commune, which took place directly after the events of the film, is alluded to only in a bitter remark by Francis: "Speaking from experience, I can say that when we stop fighting Prussians, we'll fight each other."[23]

The American scenes seem primarily aimed at demystifying and humanizing the Old West. Cowboys, gunfights, hostile Indians, and sharp moral conflicts are largely absent in Redland and Roll Point. Lelouch actually cuts away from the few moments of violence. His offbeat hero carries a gun only to shoot mortally sick or wounded animals. What remains of the Western myth is the sense of a new, individualist society slowly being born in the wilderness. The smalltown newspaper, boarding school, and photography shop are all new projects on their way to becoming institutions. Further, the French immigrants are on their way to becoming Americans. The frontier society is dangerous, as shown by the deaths of Francis and Mary. However, this is not the formulaic violence of the classic American Western, but rather the random danger of any unsettled condition.

The contrast between Europe and America works well on a purely visual level. In Paris, long lines of ragged citizens wait for the mere chance a bakery may open. Haggard, hopeless faces appear for a moment out of the darkness. Men argue in a squalid restaurant. Meanwhile, Jeanne's family gives a lavish dinner behind locked doors.

Where Paris is dank and dark, the West is characterized by glorious light. Camera filters bring out the dusty, golden quality of the light. Compositionally, Lelouch has eliminated most of the iconographic elements of the Western, substituting images based on drawings and photographs of the period. His more picturesque scenes include billiards on horseback, a communal bathhouse, and the chaotic, colorful handicap race. The attention to period detail and the lovely light combine to make the West a charmingly innocent place, the land of "another chance."

Clearly, *Another Man, Another Chance* has an ambitious thematic design. As in *And Now My Love,* individual lives intersect with great historical moments. The joys and sorrows of the lovers-to-be personalize and thus give meaning to the surrounding historical events. However, Lelouch has trouble fitting together the French and American experiences, perhaps because he tries to do too much. He wants to tell David's story, Jeanne's story, and *A Man and a Woman.* The most important of the three is Jeanne's story, which contains all the essential elements of the film: Paris in 1870, emigration, Texas, new love. Jeanne weathers every storm without changing her basic openness to experience, and thus creates a new life for herself. She is the film's central character because the transformation from France to America takes place within her. This subplot alone could have made an original and effective film.

In telling David's story, Lelouch adds many fascinating observations but greatly slows down his film. He dismantles the Western myth of a John Ford or an Anthony Mann without putting anything nearly as exciting in its place. Although David is an amusing character, his scenes are so laconic and matter-of-fact that they lose most of their drama. Lelouch certainly achieves a change of tone from the somber romanticism of Paris to the low-keyed American scenes, but only at the expense of dramatic unity. Historically as well, the film remains diffuse, an impressionist sketch rather than a probe of two societies. Loose, sprawling, filled with incident, *Another Man, Another Chance* never quite becomes a large historical epic.

The homage to *A Man and a Woman,* though certainly clever, at times interferes with the love story of David and Jeanne. For example, their courtship is notable for its understatement, its lack of obvious sentimentality. Even in the film's final moment, the characters do not embrace, they retain a certain reserve. This is an appropriate response to the nineteenth-century American setting, and it suggests that the characters may still have difficulties ahead. But the parallel to *A Man and a Woman* provides an overlay of sentiment (we remember Jean-Louis and Anne whirling around in a mad embrace) which detracts from the specific qualities of this film.

Another Man, Another Chance also has language problems. As originally shot, most of the action is in English but the Paris scenes and scenes between Jeanne and Francis are in French. The naturalistic approach to languages recalls Rossellini's *Paisan* (1946) and Godard's *Contempt* (*Le Mépris*, 1963). However, where Rossellini and Godard use language differences to show a lack of communication, Lelouch has something else in mind. He makes a few jokes on miscommunication, but he mainly uses two languages to stress cultural distinctness. He succeeds all too well. The two languages are so distinct, each being a system of thought as well as a means of communication, that it is difficult to grasp narrative connections between them. The French and American scenes appear to be two separate films. Audiences in both France and America must have been confused by this strange hybrid.

To "solve" the language problem, the film has been seen in the United States mainly in various dubbed versions.* The dubbing hurts the French scenes and destroys some cross-cultural jokes, but it does, at least, give a greater coherence to the two parallel stories.

Despite all these flaws, the performances of *Another Man, Another Chance* are generally good. James Caan is perfectly capable of being an action hero, but here he plays an extremely low-key, informal, slow-to-anger character. Awkward and blunt with people, David is devoted to his profession and actually prefers the company of animals. He often smells of the pigpen or the corral, thus demolishing any vestige of movie-star glamour. David does have the self-reliance and determination of the pioneer, but he is otherwise nonheroic. His violent scene with the bandits seems to be an instinctive and isolated reaction.[24] Caan's quiet performance as David has a wacky charm. He manages to interest us in a character who is basically very simple. The other Western characters (David's wife, the schoolteacher, the newspaper staff) are similarly provincial and sympathetic. Through them Lelouch presents an affectionate portrait of the Old West.

Genevieve Bujold plays a more complex character. Frail, childlike, and very feminine, she is well cast as a romantic heroine of the nineteenth century. However, this heroine has a bold and adventuresome spirit that connects her to Lelouch's other independent women and, indeed, to his male adventurers. Her firmly stated remark, "Je ne veux plus me marier," breaking up a very bourgeois engagement party, sets the tone for her entire story. Jeanne is self-reliant and courageous but also instinctive, trusting her emotions. Bujold is extraordinary in this role. Her flashing eyes, expressive face, and small but determined body beautifully realize the character of Jeanne. Further, although the film has language problems, Bujold, a French-Canadian, creates a memorable character in both French and English. She could probably have been more forceful and more romantic, but that would have conflicted with the quietness of the rest of the movie.

*I have seen four different versions of *Another Man, Another Chance*.

Another Man, Another Chance—Genevieve Bujold and Claude Lelouch on the set. (United Artists)

A third major character, Francis, is actually too romantic. As a desperate, starving artist, he is given to high-sounding statements about destiny and other such posturings. Francis Huster, a talented actor, has trouble bringing this character beyond stereotype. The characterization does, however, begin to make sense if one considers that the hyperromantic Francis initiates the trip West, but the more adaptable Jeanne survives it.

In addition to all its other resonances, the between-cultures theme of the film is autobiographical. *Another Man, Another Chance* is Lelouch's first primarily American film—produced by United Artists, shot mainly at Burbank Studios, and employing well-known American actors and a large Hollywood union crew. Before and during production of the film, Lelouch spoke very frankly to interviewers about being uncomfortable in France and more at ease in the United States.[25] Lelouch had several reasons for wanting to work in the United States: an affection for America and American movies dating back to his experiences in World War II and his earliest moviegoing; the greater financial and technical resources of the big American companies; and a dissatisfaction with the intellectual and critical climate in France. He was prepared to switch at least some of his film activities to the United States if *Another Man, Another Chance* was a success.

The film is not, however, a breakthrough work. It has many small virtues but lacks the action of a commercial film and the coherence of an artistic success. In attempting to universalize his appeal in an American movie, Lelouch loses some of his most important assets: rapidity, grace, control of language, and a sure sense of cultural context. *Another Man, Another Chance* failed commercially in the United States, thus ending, at least for the moment, Lelouch's plans for working there. He returned to France, where he is securely established and has a good rapport with the popular audience.

Conclusions

Lelouch's films of the mid-1970s do not have the obvious coherence of the series *The Crook–Smic–Money, Money, Money–Happy New Year*. The recent films are quite diverse in genre and style. *Le Mariage* is a bitter study of mediocrity presented in a formalized and theatrical way. *Cat and Mouse* and *Si c'était à refaire* are both pleasant genre films, the first a crime film from the detective's point of view and the second a woman's picture, combining melodrama with a view of 1970s feminism. *The Good and the Bad* is a gangster film but also a historical study. *Another Man, Another Chance* combines history with a lyrical love story.

These films could be connected with Lelouch's earlier films in a variety of ways. For example, *Cat and Mouse* and *The Good and the Bad* continue the crime cycle, and *Si c'était à refaire* and *Another Man, Another Chance* are romantic melodramas in the style of *A Man and a Woman*. *Le Mariage* could be connected with *Smic* as a low-budget experiment. Or *Le Mariage, The Good and the Bad*, and *Another Man, Another Chance* could be seen as historical films stemming from *And Now My Love*.

However, there seem to be equally valid reasons for looking at the five films from *Le Mariage* to *Another Man, Another Chance* as a group, thus continuing the chronological approach of this study. The five films exhibit at least two common features. First, the films all show an interest in moral realism. The ironic distance of the crime films is replaced by a concern with how people actually live. Lelouch takes on subjects such as hypocrisy *(Le Mariage)*, corruption *(Cat and Mouse, The Good and the Bad)*, moral relativism *(Cat and Mouse, The Good and the Bad)*, feminist morality *(Si c'était à refaire)*, and the revision of history *(Le Mariage, The Good and the Bad, Another Man, Another Chance)*. Although rarely leaving the context of entertainment, Lelouch describes a gap between conventional morality and actual behavior. For example, *The Good and the Bad* contests the notion of the French as a nation of resisters during World War II, and *Cat and Mouse* shows government corruption to be endemic and beyond control. Lelouch not only observes these failings, he philosophizes about them. The opening title of *The Good and the Bad* states the overall theme of moral relativism, and in *Cat and Mouse* Lechat's superiors calmly discuss his corruption and Lechat himself states that he was never "profoundly" with the police.

Second, moral realism is countered by another common thread of the films: optimistic, escapist storytelling. *Le Mariage* is a case apart, a uniquely pessimistic film in Lelouch's career. The other films all use familiar genre patterns treated with great verve and optimism. They are formulaic adventures in which the protagonist wins out in the end, and the refinements of Lelouch's style do not really change the inevitability of the pattern. But this lessens the impact of the moral issues that Lelouch raises. Who cares about corruption if one can live happily ever after? In *Cat and Mouse* and *Si c'était à refaire*, moral realism essentially adds a dash of spice and cynicism to films that could be very bland. It is amusing to watch Inspector Lechat uncover venality time after time with the aid of his half-trained dog. But Lelouch is much too good-natured in these two films to be seriously concerned with evil or even complication. Therefore, the films are more complacent fantasy than realist comedy or melodrama. *The Good and the Bad* and *Another Man, Another Chance* do pose important questions, but even here the optimistic formula limits Lelouch's thinking. Only *Le Mariage* works as a moral-critical film, but it sacrifices other merits of Lelouch films (mood, characterization, involvement).

It becomes clear in retrospect that the irony of Lelouch's crime film series served him very well. In those films the gangster hero is an outsider whose successful adventures take place despite a society in decline. The virtues of the outlaw point up a general mediocrity. Further, the heroes' adventures are so outlandish as to be barely plausible. Lelouch's gangster is a positive but unlikely figure in today's world. These ironies allow Lelouch to make entertaining adventures while at the same time being satirical. He is optimistic about the individual, but pessimistic about his surroundings. Irony also protects Lelouch by cutting off some possible objections to his films. For example, the violence of the movie gangster is to some extent a moot point if this character is presented as a fictional and symbolic figure.

In his films of the mid-1970's, Lelouch expresses himself more simply and directly. He tells us how he feels about government, feminism, and the United States. He is critical, but also accepting; he now evidently feels that one can live well despite corruption. The elaboration of this attitude encounters two major problems. First, Lelouch's moralizing is swallowed by an overall optimism and complacency, as noted previously. Second, topical events are greatly simplified to fit a rose-colored vision. The thoroughly corrupt world of *Cat and Mouse* causes no conflicts, and even war, in *The Good and the Bad*, is reduced at times to an amusing adventure.

In some respects Lelouch's filmmaking is better than ever. He expresses himself with great sincerity and immediacy. His excellent storytelling and technical abilities are showcased by the varied subjects of this period. He makes many acute observations. However, without irony to reconcile optimism and social criticism, the naiveté of Lelouch's ideas becomes clear. In expressing himself very directly, thus taking himself more seriously as artist and social critic, Lelouch exposes the contradictions of his thinking.

Lelouch's historical films deserve special mention. The series begins with *And Now My Love* and continues through *The Good and the Bad* and *Another Man, Another Chance*. The project of connecting the individual's adventures with the history of an entire society forces Lelouch to challenge himself, to confront new themes and situations. He deals with the interplay between public and private needs and with the sheer multiplicity of experience. He discovers a few values that modify an individual and relative morality. In *And Now My Love* the notion of family makes sense of one hundred years of experience; in *The Good and the Bad* the heroes fight for themselves and the French nation;* in *Another Man, Another Chance* the characters build a new society in both personal (family) and more general terms. Lelouch responds to the stylistic challenge of presenting history with the lyrical interweaving of several strands in *And Now My Love* and the eruption of serious choices in the comedy of *The Good and the Bad*. He does not radically change his ideas in making historical films: he indulges in easy moralizing, and he often simplifies history into fate or coincidence or genre formula. But at least the history films show that Lelouch is still ambitious, still trying to combine entertainment and experimental-critical filmmaking.

*The French nation has a positive value in *The Good and the Bad* if one believes that Jacques and his friends join the Resistance for other than totally personal and/or cynical reasons. Not only does the nation survive from 1935 to 1945, but the Resistants play an active part in its survival.

7
A Comedy and a Crime Film

Lelouch has always been a very prolific filmmaker, so it should be no surprise that in the late 1970s and early 1980s he has continued to make about one film a year. His latest works are *Robert et Robert* (1978), *A Nous deux* (1979), and *Les Uns et les autres* (1981).* These films certainly continue Lelouch's past interests, but also show him moving in new directions. *Robert et Robert* is a comedy about the lives and aspirations of two lower middle-class Parisians. The Lelouch film it most resembles, in subject and style, is *Smic, Smac, Smoc*. *A nous deux* is another Lelouch crime film, a sequel, in fact, to *The Good and the Bad*. It stands out from the other crime films, though, because of its harsher, more pessimistic tone. *Les Uns et les autres* is evidently another ambitious film in the line of *And Now My Love*. Lelouch described the film (before production) as the story of four families between 1937 and 1980, including a number of historic setpieces.[1]

Robert et Robert (1978)

Robert Villiers (Jacques Villeret) and Robert Goldman (Charles Denner) are both clients of a computer dating service–marriage bureau[2] run by M. Millet (Jean-Claude Brialy) and his wife. Villiers, in his midtwenties, is overweight, extremely shy, and without a steady job. Goldman, forty-eight, is a hawknosed, incredibly fussy cab driver. Neither can find an agreeable woman despite the best efforts of M. Millet. They make each other's acquaintance after a frustrating afternoon at the marriage bureau, and cement their friendship when both are stood up by "arranged" dates at a Saturday night dance.

Villiers eventually moves in with Goldman and his mother, sharing time driving Goldman's cab. This enrages Villiers's mother, who thinks

---

*Les Uns et les autres was shown, in competition, at the Cannes Film Festival in May 1981. It opened in New York in June, 1982 under the title *Bolero*.

Robert et Robert—Jacques Villeret as an apprentice cop. (Quartet Films)

Robert et Robert—Jacques Villeret and Charles Denner on the road to Waterloo. (Quartet Films)

the older man is a homosexual. Her misunderstanding is eventually corrected, and "Robert et Robert" continue to be fast friends.

They join other members of the marriage bureau on a weekend trip to Waterloo, which turns out to be an appropriate venue. The trip is a disaster for almost everyone, as shown by women and men sitting grimly on opposite sides of the bus on the way back. But Ali Salem, who was introduced in the scene where Robert and Robert first met, *has* found the girl of his dreams. He and his fiancée invite all those on the bus to their wedding.

In the wedding scene we suddenly switch from alienation to true community. All the lonely people, including Mme. Villiers and Mme. Goldman, join together to fete Ali and his bride. For entertainment, they take turns singing or telling jokes. When Villiers's turn comes, he mimics a conversation between himself and M. Millet, and is extremely well received. At this point Robert Goldman has a vision (daydream? flashforward?) of Villiers entertaining at a series of clubs by telling stories about his life. The series concludes with opening night at the prestigious Olympia Music Hall, a television interview, and the marriage of Villiers and the sophisticated television interviewer. Then we return to the wedding, and the newlyweds conclude the celebration by asking everyone to sing the theme from *A Man and a Woman*. After another brief flash to the Olympia, the film ends.

The theme of the film seems to be that relationships between people occur by chance and despite, rather than because of, attempts to arrange them logically. The marriage bureau's computer causes innumerable complaints throughout the film, because it insists on suggesting unattractive mates for all concerned. M. Millet, for all his charm, can do little better. But serendipitous things do happen. Robert and Robert find a true friend, and the entire group becomes a closely knit community, and Ali actually gets married. Isolated people establish some human contact, but in circuitous ways.

The film's strengths and weaknesses revolve around the attitude taken toward the characters. This fluctuates from caricature to sympathy, from distance to respect. Many elements are exaggerated. Both Roberts are presented as poor, ugly, untalented losers. Robert Villiers is so timid that he barely functions, and Robert Goldman is immensely difficult and exacting about trivial things. Both characters are so lowly in status and so extreme in their peculiarities that we sometimes laugh at them, instead of with them. Lelouch helps this along with a few scenes of forced, grimacing humor, as when Goldman deserts his cab and stumbles home after seeing a negative horoscope. Also, Mme. Goldman and Mme. Villiers are stereotyped as dominating, shrewish women, at least in relation to their sons. Several scenes deal with the stock situation of a mother's ferocity when threatened by an adult child's desertion.

On the other hand, the characters are often treated sympathetically. All of them, major and minor, are poor but respectable. They work hard, live modestly, and search for a better life. Lelouch pays considerable attention to establishing the shabby but proper milieu of petit-bourgeois Paris (graying, yellowing photography, settings without glamor but still neat and clean), and the best scenes of the film are those that come out of a sense of a real, lived-in situation. For example, the travails of the marriage bureau are presented seriously and even tenderly. All the scenes of interviewing and waiting at the marriage bureau show an understanding of the anxieties involved in meeting someone of the opposite sex. The men and women interviewed are hesitant, awkward, stubborn, and unrealistic, but none of this detracts from their essential dignity. The understated comedy here arises from a close, sympathetic observation of the characters.

The changes in attitude are never really resolved in the film. Sometimes Lelouch seems to condescend to his characters, distorting the petit bourgeoisie to make the middle class laugh. More often he treats the characters with respect and sympathy, making us care about their problems. After all, the needs these people have for affection and success should not be foreign to anyone. But occasional grating scenes and lapses of tone throw us out of this sympathetic mood.

The film's inconsistency of tone can perhaps be explained by its manner of production. *Robert et Robert* seems to be another of Lelouch's more informal films, hastily put together with the spontaneous but somewhat crude quality of a sketch. Like *Smic, Smac, Smoc, Robert et Robert* tells an anecdote of lower-class life with comic verve. Also like *Smic*, it mixes actors and nonactors in a semi-improvised context and observes their behavior very carefully.[3] But where *Smic* expressed a simple exuberance, in *Robert et Robert* Lelouch is trying to get across a more nuanced point of view. He wants us to empathize with the characters despite their obvious flaws. The style of the film, however, conflicts with this aim, since empathy requires a coherent and consistent framework.

Consider, for example, the matter of acting styles. The film features two experienced professionals (Brialy and Denner), one rising star (Villeret), and a group of unknowns or nonactors, some of whom work for Lelouch in other capacities. The mixture of styles causes certain problems. Brialy is a superb actor, but in this film he does not hold down his performance to the level of those around him. He is aristocratic, witty, and aloof, but also concerned. The role calls for a smooth talker, not for an aristocrat. Denner also seems too strong for the supporting cast. His character is aggressive, eccentric, and bizarre. Villeret, a sensitive and winning actor, is always a pleasure to watch, but a scene within the film itself shows that he could be much better. During the television interview, Villeret does his impression of an "Ingmar Bergman film," and the result is far better than anything else he does in the film. This suggests that the character of Villiers, though autobiographical (Villiers = Villeret, and the film is in part the story of Villeret's rise from humble origins to success), may not give free rein to Villeret's talent and intelligence. The other actors are at least adequate as inhabitants of the film's modest and rather bleak world, but the mix of stars and nonprofessionals does not quite work.

Another problem of tone in *Robert et Robert* is Lelouch's mania for quoting himself. He refers repeatedly to *A Man and a Woman, And Now My Love, The Good and the Bad,* and other Lelouch films. The concluding singalong of the theme from *A Man and a Woman* can be justified, since that song is by now folklore, but the other quotes are gratuitous. The problem in *Robert et Robert* is to get us involved with the situation, and the many citations to other Lelouch films take us right out of our involvement. Is Lelouch bored with his subject?

Robert et Robert is an amusing film that shows Lelouch's talent as an observer of character and setting. But the informal tone does not work as well here as it does in most of Lelouch's other films.

A nous deux (1979)

A nous deux describes the meeting of two fugitives from the law. Simon (Jacques Dutronc) is a second-generation gangster, an outlaw and enemy of the police by birth. Imprisoned for bank robbery, he escapes and makes his way to the isolated farm of Tonton Musique (Jacques Villeret), his deceased father's criminal pal. Françoise (Catherine Deneuve) is a more unusual fugitive. A pharmacist by training, she was raped in her office one night and is retaliating by seducing men, including prominent politicians, to blackmail them. She, too, comes to Tonton's farm to escape the police.

The hideout is discovered, and Tonton is brutally killed. Simon and Françoise escape together. After committing a series of ingenious crimes they take a ship to Canada in the dead of winter. Though originally Françoise wanted nothing to do with Simon, she gradually becomes interested in his intelligence, daring, and quiet charm. This is illustrated in a symbolic sense by a lovely scene of the ship breaking through an ice field. Eventually, Françoise commits herself to Simon and convinces him that he can be a success in the straight world, too. At the end of the film, the two protagonists are in an automobile junkyard (the past?) staring at the skyscrapers of Manhattan.

A nous deux is explicitly a sequel to *The Good and the Bad*. The forty-year time jump between that film (ca. 1935–45) and *A nous deux* (presumably set in the late 1970s) is skillfully handled. Dutronc plays the son of his character in the earlier film, and a heavily made-up Jacques Villeret is the aged survivor of the Front-Wheel-Drive Gang. Even Deschamps (Bruno Cremer), the police official of *The Good and the Bad,* appears in a cameo role to complain that Simon is more trouble than his father once was. Where self-citation did not work in *Robert et Robert,* the various references in this film are appropriate. These references place *A nous deux* in the tradition of *The Good and the Bad,* but the time jump and modified circumstances of the later film suggest an extension rather than repetition of Lelouch's crime genre.

There are essentially two differences between *A nous deux* and the earlier Lelouch crime films. First, the tone of the later film is grimmer and more desperate than the caper atmosphere of *The Crook* or *The Good and the Bad*. Dutronc, despite his youth, is a bleakly defiant crook with no prospects except prison and violent death. This is presented most clearly in a song he sings at the prison Christmas party, a bitter lament about the criminal's lot. The film proceeds through the death of Tonton Musique, a shocking example of the fruits of crime, to a series of adventures and a somewhat happy ending. But the adventures are more a test of skill and nerve than joyous capers, and the love story is very tentative. Symbolically, the New York of the film's last shot may be the promised land after the junkheap of crime, but the last image is still gloomy and cold. The characters' future remains uncertain.

A second difference between *A nous deux* and Lelouch's earlier films is that in this film Simon does decide to leave the world of crime. Where his father (in *The Good and the Bad*) plunged back into gangsterism after World War II, that alternative is no longer attractive to Simon. Françoise, who is basically middle class, persuades Simon that his intelligence and daring can be equally valuable in the business world. Simon's change from gangster to businessman is particularly fascinating since crime is metaphorically related to business in the earlier Lelouch films. The entrepreneur in *The Crook,* for example, became a criminal because other avenues were closed to him, and because his drive to succeed was mixed with a distrust of established institutions. Now Lelouch sees less of a need for metaphoric distance. He treats gangsterism more realistically and lets his individualist hero become a businessman. This does not, however, resolve all difficulties. At the film's end it seems clear that Simon and Françoise will continue their desperate struggle to survive, but in a new context.

The film's casting is offbeat but effective. Dutronc and Deneuve are actors of different generations and different styles. Dutronc, a relative newcomer, combines an adolescent reticence with the gangster's necessary toughness. He is a very informal actor with a rebellious, youth-culture image derived from his pop music background. Deneuve is no older than Dutronc, but she has been an established film star for nearly twenty years. Once an ingenue, she is now a calm, mature ideal of conventional, middle-class beauty. All of this is relevant to Lelouch's plot, in which the opposite natures of the characters lead first to conflict and then to a new, positive synthesis. The rebellious hero finds a new direction for his energy, and the middle-class heroine finds a way out of her private unhappiness. The same dynamic exists in other Lelouch films, but only *Happy New Year* handles it as well as *A nous deux*.

Lelouch has added one more level to the Catherine Deneuve character. Borrowing from earlier Deneuve films, especially Buñuel's *Belle de Jour* (1966), Lelouch gives her a double personality. The actress' cool exterior is countered by a concealed eroticism. Lelouch has even filmed some Buñuelian dream sequences, including the marvelous repeated image of Deneuve playing a burning cello (the rape of respectability? the burning womb?). Lelouch departs from Buñuel in showing that Deneuve's erotic side is not repressed desire but an expression of anger. Also, where the Deneuve of *Repulsion* (Roman Polanski, 1965) and *Belle de Jour* becomes increasingly schizophrenic, in this film she manages to reintegrate her personality. These variations on Deneuve's previous screen image nicely support and explain Françoise's response to Simon. Though the notion of a beautiful woman's hidden nature may be more male fantasy than psychology, Deneuve still succeeds in making this character believable.

A nous deux is one of the better Lelouch films: well written, well acted, and technically excellent. Perhaps the only criticism to make of the film is that it presents its own limitations. If the gangster's life is no longer appealing, then the importance of the adventure plot is to some extent reduced. What happens after the ending may be more interesting than what has gone before.

8
Lelouch and the New Wave

At various points in this study Claude Lelouch's work has been related to the films of several of France's leading filmmakers: Jean-Luc Godard, François Truffaut, Alain Resnais, Eric Rohmer, and others. Such connections run contrary to most critical thinking today, where Godard, Truffaut, Rohmer, Resnais, and a few others are considered part of the very significant French New Wave, whereas Lelouch is labeled a commercial filmmaker and ignored. However, these critical boundaries are too narrow, and a great deal can be learned by connecting Lelouch to the New Wave. The next two chapters sketch out this relationship, first in terms of style and method, then in terms of content.

Historically, the term "nouvelle vague" was applied to all the new French films and filmmakers of the late 1950s and early 1960s, a period of extraordinary cinematic creativity. At this time more than two hundred filmmakers directed a first feature film, with at least a few dozen of them attracting critical attention to the excellence and originality of their work. Recent books in English have tended to limit the New Wave to a small group of directors with a background in film criticism: Godard, Truffaut, Rohmer, Claude Chabrol, and Jacques Rivette.[1] Resnais is sometimes added to the group because he is too important to omit. This grouping has the advantage of coherence, since these directors all knew each other and had worked together on the magazine *Cahiers du Cinéma* (hereafter *Cahiers*) plus a variety of short film projects.[2] But this list does not mention Louis Malle, Agnès Varda, Jacques Demy, Jacques Rozier, Jean Rouch, Chris Marker, Jacques Doniol-Valcroze, Jean-Pierre Mocky, Claude Lelouch, and other gifted young directors of the late 1950s and early 1960s. Even though these directors are not necessarily linked by background and friendships, they share with the *Cahiers* group, and with each other, some basic attitudes and methods of filmmaking.[3] The following analysis of Lelouch illustrates the ideas and methods that connect this loosely defined group.

In the French film world of the 1970s and 1980s the New Wave cannot be regarded as a movement, but the ideas and directors of 1958–

63 remain highly influential. Thus, a discussion of the New Wave's nature and composition is not purely a historical exercise. It has a great deal of relevance to the present as well.

Relating Lelouch to the New Wave represents only one possible critical approach. In some respects Lelouch's cinema may have more to do with the light comedies of Philippe de Broca (*King of Hearts*, 1966; *Dear Inspector*, 1978), Yves Robert (*The Tall Blond Man with One Black Shoe*, 1972; *Pardon mon affaire*, 1976), and Jean-Claude Tacchella (*Cousin, Cousine*, 1976) than with Godard or Resnais. Connections between Lelouch and various trends in American cinema might also be pursued. But the point of connecting Lelouch to the New Wave is not to proclaim identity. It is, rather, to illuminate both terms of the comparison by establishing a significant relationship between them.

The key theoretical notion behind the new French film circa 1960 was the "cinéma d'auteur," the idea that the director was or should be the author of a film. This idea, as advanced by Truffaut, Rivette, Godard, and other critics writing in *Cahiers* in the 1950s, had both critical and practical components. The critical component proposed that film history and criticism should be primarily concerned with directors. The *Cahiers* critics felt that a good director was able to impose his artistic personality on a film even if he worked within a collaborative, studio system. Therefore, film criticism should study the thematic and stylistic qualities of a director's work. The practical component of the theory was an analysis of French film industry conditions and of the prerequisites of artistic filmmaking. Truffaut, who took the lead here, suggested that low-budget but artistically ambitious films could be made in the French film industry. He further suggested that one person should both write and direct a film.[4] A film auteur could function in a studio situation, but ideally the director-auteur should have complete artistic control over his work.

The "cinéma d'auteur" was put into practice by many young filmmakers in the late 1950s and early 1960s. Taking advantage of a slump in traditional French production, they wrote, directed, and often produced and financed their own low-budget films. Though sometimes lacking in craft, these films were full of energy and new ideas. Most of them, including the early efforts of Claude Lelouch, were critical and financial failures. However, Truffaut, Godard, Resnais, Chabrol, and a few others directed artistically and financially successful films that made the cinéma d'auteur a viable alternative to commercial production. The auteur-based cinema has since spread around the world.

Lelouch has been a film auteur since the beginning of his career. He writes, directs, produces, and photographs each of his films. His production company, Les Films 13, is also active in financing, publicity, and distribution. Lelouch does have collaborators: Alexandre Mnouchkine the producer, Pierre Uytterhoeven the writer, Tania Zazulinsky the all-purpose executive, Arlette Gordon the publicist-assistant director, and others with whom he has worked for years.* One man does not make a film company. However, this company is set up to make one man's films. Lelouch is involved at every stage and he makes the final decisions. His multiple activities are very demanding but they give him a great deal of independence and control in filmmaking.

Lelouch's films are excellent examples of personal style. Everything in his films is distinctive: story, visual style, acting, themes, music. All of Lelouch's films are based on original scripts and they are unique experiences except in relation to each other. Audiences come to see "a film by Claude Lelouch," a very personal communication between director and viewer. Uniqueness does not make Lelouch a great artist, but it does mark him as a film auteur.

The main limit on Lelouch's freedom is, of course, the marketplace. He can only make films as long as people will go to see them. This may not be a tremendous problem, since Lelouch wants to please a large public and he has a flair for doing so. The marketplace does, however, create an interesting tension in Lelouch's work. On the one hand, economics suggests that he repeat himself to maintain an audience. If *Happy New Year* worked, *Cat and Mouse* should also be successful. The auteur's signature is also a brand name, encouraging sameness. On the other hand, the artist is supposed to be creative. "Etonnez-nous," says the public. Lelouch is actually successful enough so that he can take an occasional gamble *(And Now My Love)* or experiment with a low-budget film *(Smic, Le Mariage)*.

One consequence of the "cinéma d'auteur" is a greater emphasis on visual style. If the director is the author of a movie, special attention will naturally be paid to directing. For the French, the director's specific responsibility is mise-en-scène, which refers primarily to the visual organization of the film (direction of actors, dialogue, and sound may also be involved). Thus, auteur criticism centers on how meaning is created by visual style, and auteur cinema tries to create meaning through style. Directors like Godard, Truffaut, Resnais, Varda, and Demy use innovative approaches to such elements as shot selection, composition, lighting, camera movement, movement within the frame, and color symbolism to get their ideas across.

Lelouch is as flamboyant a stylist as one will find among film directors. With his training in filming Scopitones and documentaries, Lelouch often tries to pull the maximum visual impact from a scene. His camera is constantly zooming, tracking, circling, and ascending, which

---

*Alexandre Mnouchkine often serves as line producer, leaving Lelouch free to concentrate on directing. Lelouch remains the executive producer, in fact if not in title. Pierre Uytterhoeven often cowrites a script with Lelouch.

creates a dynamic and emotional effect. Lelouch is capable, though, of shooting quiet scenes that foreground the actor's work. His technical repertoire also extends from the documentarylike realism of hand-held cameras, location shooting, and loose framing to the stylization of brilliant colors, monochrome tints, and cutting to music. This outgoing but sensitive style involves the audience in Lelouch's ideas and points to the director's creative work.

Lelouch departs from almost all feature film directors, New Wave or not, by acting as his own cameraman. These two functions of filmmaking are generally separated so that the director can supervise all aspects of production, leaving the camera work to a competent specialist. Lelouch does employ a director of photography to handle the difficult and time-consuming task of lighting, but he feels that composition, framing, and camera movement are too crucial to the meaning of a film to be left to someone else. He comments, "Would Van Gogh let somebody else hold his brush?"[5]

Given Lelouch's stylistic approach, it does make sense for the director to be the cameraman. The slightly pretentious analogy to Van Gogh calls attention to Lelouch's interest in the process and texture of filmmaking. He relies very heavily on the physical qualities of the visual image—color, duration, movement, depth—to give meaning to his films. For example, Lelouch typically uses a series of very rapid camera movements to provide a feeling of exhilaration. The camera movements are not just embellishments, they are often as important as the objects being photographed. This kind of stylistic nuance would be difficult to delegate. Further, by hand-holding the camera, Lelouch establishes an intimate, personal relationship with his characters. Subtle movements and reframings can bring out the details the director wants.

Lelouch has often been criticized, especially in France, for his extravagant visual style. He is accused of virtuosity for virtuosity's sake. This is not strictly true; every camera move has a thematic point. Occasionally we see a camera technique out of all proportion to its context, but only because a scene has failed. In *Si c'était à refaire*, enormous zooms destroy the scene in which Catherine meets Patrick. In *And Now My Love* the death of the Romanoffs is marred by the camera's swooping back and forth (to create suspense?). In *Happy New Year* a scene of Françoise cleaning up for Simon becomes a demonstration of how rapidly a camera can move around a circular floor plan. These scenes are all the result of Lelouch trying to do something extraordinary with the camera. One could match them with many examples of successful camera techniques.

Another important characteristic of the New Wave is a new informality and spontaneity of filmmaking. This shift is partly the result of production conditions. Many of the New Wave directors had previously

Claude Lelouch at work. *A Man and a Woman*. (Allied Artists)

Un Homme qui me plaît. With Alexandre Mnouchkine *(left)* and Jean-Paul Belmondo *(right)*. (Academy of Motion Picture Arts and Sciences)

And Now My Love. Setting up the opening scene. (Academy of Motion Picture Arts and Sciences)

Another Man, Another Chance. With James Caan and Alexandre Mnouchkine. (United Artists)

worked in documentary films, and the demands of low-budget features encouraged them to retain techniques such as location shooting, narration, and the use of nonactors. Informality is just as much a consequence of a change in attitude. The New Wave filmmakers are looking for a more personal relationship with the spectator. So, instead of creating an "objective" cinematic realism with the director absent from his work, the New Wave auteurs stress immediacy, spontaneity, and various methods of directly or indirectly addressing the audience. Many of their films have autobiographical subjects and familiar settings. Improvisation and hand-held cameras bring the spectator closer to the characters. The director puts himself in the film through narration, quotes, personal appearances, and style that calls attention to itself. Often the process of making the film is in some way included in the filmmaking product.

Unlike some New Wave directors who abandoned the informality of their first films when they began working with higher budgets, Lelouch organizes his films to ensure simplicity, informality, and spontaneity. His technical collaborators are old friends, many of them employed full time by Les Films 13. On the set, they intuitively understand what the director wants. This allows Lelouch to work very quickly, so that actors and technicians can get caught up in the rhythm of production. Working this way also encourages a warm, relaxed mood during filming, which is exactly the mood Lelouch wants reflected on the screen.

Lelouch builds informality into his work in several ways. Most of the films are autobiographical or set in milieus the director knows well (news reporting, pop music, upper-bourgeois Paris). Narration is often used to intervene between image and spectator, although Lelouch rarely speaks himself or appears on screen. Certain actors participate in film after film, suggesting that the films are products of an artisanal group or a family. Lelouch's favorites include professional actors (Charles Denner, Jacques Villeret, Charles Gérard) and technicians doubling in small roles (Jean Collomb, Jacques Lefrançois, Elie Chouraqui, Arlette Gordon). Lelouch's films are also full of jokes and references to films in general and to Lelouch's work in particular. The nature and process of cinema is a subtext of *A Man and a Woman*, *Live for Life*, *Un Homme qui me plaît*, and *And Now My Love*.

Lelouch's most elaborate technique for encouraging informality and spontaneity in his films involves the direction of actors. His method has not radically changed since *A Man and a Woman*. The actors still do not see a completed script. Lelouch gives them their dialogue day by day, and they discover its context in the process of shooting. If a scene is not working, Lelouch will add a character, change dialogue, change movement, or do something similar to restore spontaneity. However, Lelouch's current style of long takes and complicated stories, quite different from the fragmented montage of *A Man and a Woman*, requires certain alterations of this method. The actors must be instructed more thoroughly, and the technical aspects of long takes must be worked out more elaborately. Lelouch feels that he improvises much less now than he did in his early films.[6] It might be more correct to say that the focus of improvisation has changed. In *A Man and a Woman* the crucial decision was which image to record. The director-cameraman made a kind of documentary of the actor's responses. In *Happy New Year* or *Si c'était à refaire*, improvisation lies in the interaction between actor and cameraman while the camera is running.

Lelouch's semi-improvised approach to acting generally works very well. He has had a few failures, but in most cases he develops a rapport with his actors and is able to sustain a subtle emotional tone throughout a film. There is more detail of feeling, more complicated interaction between characters in Lelouch's movies than in almost any others. This should not, however, be seen as a claim that Lelouch's films are more realistic than others, since a film is not just freshness in acting but also plot and structure. The semi-improvised acting makes more sense as a thematic device. It highlights a few emotions that recur throughout Lelouch's films: timidity, warmth, friendship, resourcefulness. Further, the actor creating his role in midshot corresponds strikingly to the typical Lelouch protagonist who must find himself and improvise his life.

Lelouch's approach to directing actors seems revolutionary, but it is actually not unique. The late Jean Renoir, for example, is well known for the freedom of interpretation he gave his actors within a preestablished context.[7] Among Lelouch's contemporaries, Godard, in the 1960s, told his actors their dialogue only at the last minute to encourage a fresh response. Rivette has the actors participate in developing their characters and putting together a story in the course of production. The director who is most strikingly parallel to Lelouch is documentarist Jean Rouch. Where some critics and filmmakers fear that filming any real event will distort it, Rouch feels that the camera acts as a catalyst to reveal truths that are normally hidden. Therefore, Rouch challenges and provokes the subjects of his films with his camera. He finds that putting his "characters" in a situation where they have to respond to the camera makes them reveal far more about themselves than they normally would.[8] Lelouch is trying to obtain a similar effect in fiction. By working at the interface between controlled and uncontrolled performance, he tries to get an honest and deeply felt response from his actors.

Clearly, Claude Lelouch belongs to the New Wave in stylistic terms. A question that is still to be answered, though, is whether he shares the basic attitude toward film of that loosely defined movement. What is cinema, and what should it be used for? The New Wave is known as a radical, contestatory, and intellectual film movement. New Wave films suggest that the feature film should be not just an entertainment but a means of exploring both the world and the art of cinema. Lelouch, on the other hand, occasionally makes statements like this: "I only believe in pleasure . . . I am not trying to make films that will stay in the history of cinema; I only want to amuse the people who will go and see the films tomorrow morning."[9]

Lelouch himself has no desire to be grouped with the New Wave or any movement. He is very jealous of his independence and denies being influenced by any French cinema.* He regards the New Wave as an intellectual, elitist cinema that ignores the mass public. He prefers the American cinema, a cinema that "respects the public."[10]

Despite these distinctions, there is quite a bit of common ground between Lelouch and his contemporaries on the questions of what cinema is and should be. The New Wave directors had a broad and thorough film education based on Paris's unique film-cultural institutions: the Cinémathèque Française, the Art and Essay theaters, the commercial theaters, the cine-clubs, the film magazines. They were cinema pluralists, admiring the popular American cinema as much as the French tradition of Vigo, Renoir, Cocteau, and Bresson. When they turned to making films, these young enthusiasts tried to use all the cinema's potential, to combine popular appeal with artistic self-expression. They thus inherited the project of Griffith, Chaplin, Eisenstein, Lang, Renoir, Welles, and the other great directors of the past.

Going a step further, the New Wave found that one film could have pluralistic meanings and audience appeals. A gangster film could also be a love story, a parody, a personal commentary by the director and a reflection on the nature of cinema. A film could be formalistic, concerned with its own organization, and realistic, aimed outward at the real world, and entertaining, giving pleasure to the audience. Working on several levels at once, the New Wave tried to combine spectacle and art.

The New Wave directors did not set out to make intellectual, avant-garde films. They filmed subjects that interested and moved them, hoping that the public would also be interested. However, the self-consciousness and the artistic ambitions of these directors ensured that their films would differ from what had gone before. The best New Wave films are full of challenging ideas and new connections. They require critical awareness as well as emotional empathy from the spectator. Therefore, the New Wave has become a type of art film, aimed primarily at an elite audience.

Still, the diversity of cinematic experience, the need for spectacle as

*Personal relationships have to be considered here. Lelouch was not friendly with the *Cahiers* group in the 1960s, and he was panned by the magazine. Why, then, would he want to be lumped together with the *Cahiers* directors?

well as analysis, remains central to the New Wave aesthetic. Truffaut once described cinema as a "show," a "circus," and a "music hall," all popular media in which it is necessary to orchestrate the audience's attention.[11] The austere and rigorous Resnais has a vivid interest in popular culture—science fiction, comic strips, melodrama—and in film as spectacle. The problem of such directors is to follow a personal line of development while maintaining contact with the public. Artistic achievement need not preclude the audience's pleasure.

In the early 1960s, the New Wave directors shared a rough consensus of film style. All of them made personal, experimental films within more or less conventional narratives. This consensus has since broken down. Some directors (Godard, Rivette) have moved toward the experimental. Others (Truffaut, Chabrol) have become more conventional. Louis Malle alternates mass audience films (*Murmur of the Heart, Pretty Baby*) with less commercial projects (*Phantom India, Black Moon*). Alain Resnais has continued his own unique approach to filmmaking, collaborating every few years with writers such as Marguerite Duras, Alain Robbe-Grillet, and David Mercer. The current dispersion provides an index of the fruitful mix of possibilities of the New Wave's early years.

Lelouch fits onto the entertainment end of the New Wave spectrum. He believes very strongly in film as mass entertainment, but also believes that film can be something more. Lelouch says that his goal is to make a film that is both "popular" and of "great quality," both "generous" and "noble," both a "commercial film" and a "festival film."[12] Lelouch's description of *The Good and the Bad* gives a good idea of the multiple levels of his films: "My objective was more anecdotal than historical and I also wanted to make a contemporary work, a comedy offering good humor and which can cause reflection in making people laugh."[13] The typically down-to-earth metaphor of a menu is another means Lelouch uses to describe how one film can please different publics.

Incidentally, Lelouch's comments on his films generally assume an auteur cinema. Lelouch defines his basic goals and chooses the means of achieving them. The idea, still very important in American films, that a director interprets a script or property or subject simply does not apply.

Like Godard (of the 1960s) and Truffaut, Lelouch relies heavily on the mixture of genres. Many of his films are a combination of love story, adventure film, comedy, topical film, and personal communication. Starting from familiar conventions, he confronts, combines, and complicates genres to get at his own unique view of the world. In the process he has created a new genre, the Claude Lelouch film, just as Chabrol and Hitchcock have staked out territories in the mystery-thriller.

Lelouch is certainly less of a critical intellectual than Godard or Resnais or Rivette. Except for the slightly avant-garde *Le Mariage*, Lelouch has always stayed close to the entertainment aspect of cinema. However, he does use the cinema for more than pure diversion. His films present a personal vision and provide a forum for the director's attitudes. He shares the New Wave's commitment to the richness and diversity of cinematic communication.

9
Alienation and Happiness

The New Wave has usually been discussed in stylistic terms, but it also has a thematic consistency. Most of the New Wave films are about small groups of marginal, isolated, young people. Whether students, workers, bohemians, or even middle-class professionals, the characters share a feeling of estrangement from their society. The films avoid large, heroic subjects and present negative views of great social institutions—work, politics, the family, conventional morality—if they consider them at all. In a word, these are alienation films. The description applies to an amazingly wide variety of films: youth films (*The 400 Blows*, Truffaut, 1959), gangster films (*Breathless*, Godard, 1959), love stories (*A Man and a Woman*, Lelouch, 1966), science fiction (*Je t'aime, je t'aime*, Resnais, 1968), crime films (*A Double Tour*, Chabrol, 1960), comedies (*A Woman Is a Woman*, Godard, 1960), adaptations of novels (*La Tête contre les murs*, directed by Georges Franju, screenplay by Jean-Pierre Mocky, 1958), plus unique films such as *Hiroshima mon amour* (Resnais, 1959) and *Jules and Jim* (Truffaut, 1962). The New Wave extends from the romances of Lelouch and Demy to the avant-garde films of Alain Robbe-Grillet and Marguerite Duras, and from the ultraconservatives of *Le Feu follet* (Malle, 1963) to the Maoists of *La Chinoise* (Godard, 1967).

The concept of alienation describes the effects of the tremendous social dislocations brought about by industrialization and modernization. The concept originates with Karl Marx, who analyzes the industrial worker's estrangement from both the product and the process of his labor. Similar splits between individuals and huge social institutions occur in government, private bureaucracies, the marketplace, mass communications, and, indeed, everyday life in the modern city. The assembly line can serve as a paradigm of how the individual's personal relationship with the essentials of his life (nature, other people, work) has been increasingly replaced by a structured impersonality and isolation. Mediating instruments such as family, church, and subculture have lost much of their influence because they cannot control the "megastructures."[1] Further, the individual is fragmented because work, government, and private life make very different demands on him. The term *alienation* refers to this whole process and more specifically to its social-psychological effects.

For our purposes here, it is important to note that industrialization and modernization are not one-time processes. Instead, the pace of technological and (related) social change is continuing and actually accelerating. Affluence increases with this continuing change; people live better materially. But alienation also increases. Thus, it is a key area of inquiry not only for Marx, observing the transformations of the mid-nineteenth century, but for contemporary sociology as well. In France after World War II, a period of extremely rapid social change, Henri Lefebvre describes the situation like this: " New types of alienations have joined ranks with the old, enriching the typology of alienation: political, ideological, technological, bureaucratic, urban, etc."[2] Some examples of the "new alienations" are consumerism and advertising, which structure previously private areas of experience, and a politics dominated by two distant superpowers (the notion of a vague "power" being itself an example of alienated thinking). Godard, speaking in the mid-1960s, comments that "The French today are suddenly waking up to the extraordinary transformations in their life and society, and they are not really adapted to it at all, they're like children."[3] The New Wave films are a reaction to this uneasy situation.

Two factors contributing to alienation in the post-World War II period are of special relevance to the New Wave. The first is the creation of a youth identity or "youth culture" in France and other industrialized countries after World War II. Young people are very susceptible to alienation because they have no strong roots in the past. In a period of accelerated change their parents' experiences have no connection to the children's lives—thus creating the celebrated "generation gap."[4] Youth gains an identity of its own, based on the present, and becomes aware of its powerlessness. Power is held by older people, and by impersonal, half-understood institutions. The youth identity is intensified by affluence, which creates such possibilities as prolonged adolescence and a market of youthful consumers.

A second relevant factor is the "disarray"[5] of French intellectuals after World War II. Dreams of a cultural and spiritual renaissance stemming from the Resistance quickly faded as France returned to prewar patterns. Existentialism, the dominant intellectual movement of the immediate postwar period, failed to provide a coherent program of action. Intellectuals were being displaced from their role as the arbiters and critics of French society by a new group, the technocrats (engineers, social scientists, managers). Further, intellectuals of the Left faced a series of political crises that they were powerless to control: the cold war, decolonization, the Algerian War, de Gaulle's autocratic Fifth Republic, the split between political parties of the French Left. The responses to these problems included not only a pessimistic, alienated world view but also attempts to find a certain autonomy or control in art.[6]*

The New Wave combines these two strands of dissatisfaction. It is a cinema made by alienated young intellectuals and intended primarily for a young, intellectual audience. The mixture of these factors varies from film to film. Some films are mainly high-spirited, confused, anarchistic expressions of youth, and others stress the lucid pessimism of the intellectual.

Given a situation of alienation, the crucial question becomes: How does one get out of it? How does one retrieve happiness, meaningfulness, some degree of control? The New Wave films of the period around 1960 find this "counteralienation" mainly in private life. With society rapidly changing and norms breaking down, only private life remains comprehensible and attractive. In fact, private freedoms have increased with the decline of mediating structures such as the family. New Wave films experiment with new life-styles and celebrate the present moment. They counterpose the joys of the couple and of friendship to the anxieties of the larger world.

The privatist solution is not exactly radical, since most popular films and novels find a happy ending in private life. But the best New Wave films do not bask in contentment. They describe the meaninglessness of modern life, rebel against it, and analyze the limits and options of privatist rebellion. Jean Pivasset describes the dominant characteristic of this cinema as "lucidity,"[7] the attempt to understand. One could also point to the quality of "searching" in these films. The solution of private life is itself open to question.

Alienation is an important theme of Lelouch's films of the 1960s, but it becomes less important in his films after 1970. He begins with the isolation of youth in a meaningless world. The hero of *Le Propre de l'homme,* played by young Claude Lelouch, is the loneliest, most timid, and most depressed character in any Lelouch film. The hero of *L'Amour avec des si* is almost as depressed. In both fims, only private life exists. *Une Fille et des fusils* adds the elements of work and the group of friends, but its heroes reject factory work and the gang is ultimately torn

---

*What does this have to do with Lelouch, who is quite simply not a French intellectual of the traditional type? One could argue that the tendency to regard filmmakers as authorities on life, love, and politics is a consequence of the failures of other intellectuals. Lelouch satirizes this tendency in *And Now My Love,* but at other points in his films and in interviews he seems to take the role of seer and authority quite seriously.

apart by outside pressures. These films are told from a young person's viewpoint, and they have a simplicity and irreverence that are analogous to pop music.

The films of the late 1960s can be analyzed in pairs. *Live for Life* and *Life, Love, Death* are clearly films of social alienation. François Toledo's powerlessness is mirrored by his impotence and frustration with prostitutes. When imprisoned, he loses whatever shred of freedom and dignity he once had. Robert, in *Live for Life*, has a more comfortable, middle-class existence, but his life, too, is fragmented and out of control. Both films tie social dislocations—the gap between the assembly line and affluence, or between political violence and love—to individual problems. *A Man and a Woman* and *Un Homme qui me plaît*, on the other hand, are principally love stories. It takes a bit of interpretation to see that they might be social as well as personal dramas, that the extreme isolation of the first and the artificial situation (tourism) of the second are related to alienation. *A Man and a Woman* is based on the idea that Anne has no resources (family, church, friends) that can console her after the death of her husband. Close personal relationships are rare and almost irreplaceable. In *Un Homme qui me plaît*, the tourist's superficial, commoditized relationship to the places he visits colors every aspect of the film, including the film-within-a-film the actors are working on and their love story. In all four films the characters are groping for a solution.

We have already mentioned that these films provide considerable compensations for alienation: glamor, material pleasures, love affairs. More generally, it seems that Lelouch never completely abandons a certain comic spirit. Even his most depressed characters retain a capacity for enjoyment, and a sense of life as possibility is constant in his work. In *L'Amour avec des si* and *Une Fille et des fusils*, a series of gags suggests the high spirits of youth and gives the films a light tone. The films beginning with *A Man and a Woman* are not specifically humorous, but they can be considered comic in the sense proposed by Susanne Langer: "Comedy is an art form that arises naturally wherever people are gathered to celebrate life . . . it is an image of human vitality holding its own in the world amid the surprises of unplanned coincidence."[8] *A Man and a Woman*, *Live for Life*, and *Une Homme qui me plaît* are, among other things, demonstrations of resilience and vitality in the modern world. Despite real problems, the characters find each other and move toward happiness in an exciting, sometimes spectacular environment. Lelouch regards even *Life, Love, Death* as a positive film; the death of Toledo brings out the importance and preciousness of life.[9]

Lelouch's perspective on the contemporary scene is therefore double. On the one hand, he is sensitive to the problems of alienation; on the other hand, he sees happiness as still possible and perhaps enhanced by affluence and rapid change. The flashy, high-powered montage construction of the films beginning with *A Man and a Woman* shows the contradictory pulls (attraction-repulsion) of modernity very well. At one level this visual style simply presents the glamor and excitement of modern life. It is very close to the style of commercials, which is not surprising considering Lelouch's previous background. But the glamorous surfaces and fragmented montages of his films of the late 1960s also give a sense of superficiality and confusion. Insofar as they are subjective styles, they show characters who are unable to understand and integrate their surroundings. In this same period other filmmakers, notably Godard and Antonioni, were using styles based on advertising (brilliant colors, simple compositions, shallowness of image) to indicate lack of depth, lack of connection, and lack of humanness. Lelouch seems to be using both the original and the secondary meanings of the style.[10]

Lelouch's films of the late 1960s draw more on youthful rebellion than on intellectual analysis, although they do attempt to understand the social setting, and *Live for Life* is specifically about an alienated intellectual. The heroes of these films are older than in the previous period, perhaps to universalize their appeal, but the subject matter is still confusion, isolation, romance, and restlessness.[11] Stylistically as well, Lelouch's dynamic approach evokes the energy and sensitivity of youth. The pull between alienation and modern glamor might also express a youthful attitude (unease plus expectation), but it could fit the average, universal spectator equally well. For spectators less conscious of alienation than the intellectual or the disaffected youth, Lelouch's mixture of modern discontents with middle-class affluence plus escapist glamor should be very attractive. It manages to be contemporary and romantic at the same time. The enormous success of *A Man and a Woman* attests to the appeal of this mixture.

After 1969 the alienated individual becomes less prominent in Lelouch's films. *And Now My Love* describes adolescent confusion and isolation in an affluent setting, but the film is mainly a *Bildungsroman*, a story of growth. It is therefore more open and optimistic than Lelouch's works of the 1960s. In *Si c'était à refaire* the flashback explaining Catherine's prison term (her alienation) seems added on, foreign to the rest of the film. The crime films do not particularly stress the angst of the gangster, and in *Cat and Mouse* life is wonderful at both the beginning and the end. The "average Frenchmen" of *Le Mariage*, *The Crook*, and other films are still frustrated and unhappy, and *Money, Money, Money* shows that individual freedom is threatened in the modern world. But on balance, the 1970s films are overwhelmingly optimistic.

Lelouch has switched his emphasis from the problem of alienation to its solution. How can one be happy in the modern world? Lelouch suggests four main solutions: love, friendship, work, and adventure.

Love, which transcends all problems in *A Man and a Woman*, is only one part of a full, happy life in the films of the 1970s. It is still, however, the closest possible bond between two people, and thus compensates for a general impersonality. Friendship, another close bond, provides a way to face the world day by day. It offers solidarity and the ability to laugh together, to take things lightly. Factory work is alienating for Lelouch (*Une Fille et des fusils, Life, Love, Death, Smic*), but he also presents many independent, often entrepreneurial jobs that are a means of challenging life and asserting one's identity. This kind of work is a common endeavor taken on by friends, and the process is more important than the results. Most fundamental of all is adventure, a situation in which imagination and daring can accomplish great things. Like Lelouch's filmmaking style, adventure involves not only planning but also improvisation, the ability to live and act in the unpredictable present.

Lelouch has essentially expanded New Wave privatism to solve all the problems of alienation. He deals very specifically with such issues as isolation, powerlessness, and self-estrangement. Characters gain identity and solidarity by forming into small groups. Work and private life are reunited and seen as a varied whole. Activity gives the individual some power to shape, or at least influence, his life (Lelouch does not dwell on the political implications of this idea). When love, friendship, work, and adventure are combined, an immanent happiness becomes possible. The searching quality of a film such as *Live for Life* is largely replaced by a delight in activity (*The Good and the Bad*) or a kind of serenity (*Cat and Mouse*), both of which are seen as ends in themselves. The dominant mood is comic and at times pastoral.

Stylistically, Lelouch supports this picture of happiness very well. He surrounds his characters with simple pleasures: sunlight, music, laughter, a good meal. The fragmented montage of the 1960s films is replaced by long takes, expressing continuity, and the shallowness of the image yields to greater depth, especially in pastoral films like *Smic* and *Another Man, Another Chance*.* The dynamism of Lelouch's style is now carried mainly by camera movement. Other techniques—the "true" emotional response produced by semiimprovised acting, the intimacy of the hand-held camera, the attention to nuances of feeling—aim at making the characters convincing. Despite certain weaknesses (blandness, oversimplification), Lelouch does succeed in creating a powerful image of a full, happy life. In films such as *Happy New Year* and *And Now My Love*, every detail of the mise-en-scène illuminates the pursuit of happiness, and even in his less successful films Lelouch gets his characteristic theme and mood across.

---

*The earlier style does linger, however, in *The Crook* and *And Now My Love*, two films where alienation must still be overcome.

The myth of happiness in this group of films can be interpreted in two very different ways. First, it has a strong escapist side. Lelouch provides a simple picture of happiness as compensation for the more difficult lives people actually live, and he proposes that one can live well in this world, without changing it. Politics is crooked and incomprehensible, and thus should be avoided. Instead, people should pursue private goals. Lelouch tends to omit complications—for example, the betrayal of a friend, or the barriers of social class—which would contradict this view. The light tone of his films, so attractive in itself, often glosses over important issues. The limits of Lelouch's ideas are made particularly clear by his various attempts to generalize them. For example, what would happen if everyone behaved like the gangsters of *The Crook* and *Money, Money, Money*? According to *And Now My Love*, the result would be the wonderful land of the United States, where people do outrageous things to achieve individual happiness. It seems not to occur to Lelouch that gangsterism (or extreme individualism, if the gangster is only a metaphor) might have a negative social cost. Even *The Good and the Bad* significantly underplays the disastrous consequences of having a gangster, Lafont, in power.[12] The myth of happiness is effective on the level of immediate, emotional response. However, as an argument or theory it is far from adequate.

Lelouch's recent films are more interesting as entertaining and in-structive comedies on what an ideal hero might be. Some films (*The Crook, Smic,* and *Money, Money, Money*) develop a biting satire from the gap between a fantasy of mastering the world and harsh reality. In *Money, Money, Money*, the individual is still robust, but the world has gone crazy. Other films simply present the qualities and successes of Lelouch's heroes. These films have an element of escapism, but they also convey the values of love, friendship, work, and adventure, and related attributes (independence, courage, generosity, imagination, daring). The films suggest that with those qualities one can make a start at an active, creative, and happy life. The lighthearted, adventuresome mood that Lelouch communicates so well, a mood of both pleasure and creative discovery, gives an inkling of what this life might be. The filmmaker's somewhat pessimistic or cynical view of the average man and the contemporary scene gives added force to his instructive mes-sage. Lelouch thus provides, through the traditional form of the adven-ture film, a (partial) solution to alienation, and a (partial) critique of how people actually live.

The rebelliousness of youth has receded a bit in Lelouch's films of the 1970s, although he retains a romantic outlook and stylistically he is still energetic and daring. A film like *And Now My Love*, which attempts to understand the entire twentieth century, shows that an intellectual component also remains in his work. However, the element of pleasure, which was always part of Lelouch's films, now becomes paramount. He presents a dream of happiness which a very broad audience can share.

With this dream of happiness Lelouch's films show a striking resemblance to the light comedies of de Broca, Robert, and Tacchella. Alienation becomes little more than a convention, a comic complication. In Lelouch's films, as in the others' comedies, characters lead extraordinarily pleasant lives. They rarely suffer grievous harm, and when that does happen they quickly bounce back. The death of Francis in *Another Man, Another Chance*, the rape of Catherine in *Si c'était à refaire*, and the desertion of the mentally unstable Karine (Marie-France Pisier) in *Cousin, Cousine* are all compensated by the sense that life continues, happiness is around the corner. Serious crimes in *Cat and Mouse, Dear Inspector*, and *The Tall Blond Man with One Black Shoe* are less important than the pleasures of courtship. The future may be uncertain in *Happy New Year* and *Cousin, Cousine*, but one lives well for the duration of an affair.

These films do have a component of social criticism, since the "good life" presented in them is more adventuresome than that of the average spectator. They encourage the viewer to at least contemplate life patterns that are somewhat outside the norm—for example, the independent women of *Happy New Year* and *Dear Inspector*, or the casual romances of *Cat and Mouse* and *Pardon mon affaire*. Annette Insdorf suggests that films such as *Get Out Your Handkerchiefs* (Bertrand Blier, 1978), *Pardon mon affaire, Cousin, Cousine, La Cage aux Folles*, and *Cat and Mouse* are popular in the United States precisely because they propose a more tolerant and adventuresome attitude toward sexual behavior, thus countering American puritanism. However, she hastily adds that this approach to social criticism is notably mild and unthreatening.[13]

In contrast to the rose-colored view of the light comedies, films such as *Jules and Jim* (Truffaut, 1962), *Pierrot le fou* (Godard, 1965), *Lacombe, Lucien* (Malle, 1973), and *Providence* (Resnais, 1977) include the possibilities of pain, loss, and irreconcilable error. These films have their moments of happiness, too, but they are more realistic and more nuanced in their view of human behavior than those of the "charm school."[14] Even a delightful comedy like Truffaut's *Stolen Kisses* (1968) ends with the introduction of an obsessive stranger to show the dangers and complexities of experience. The films of Godard, Resnais, Truffaut, and others remain true to the New Wave goal of lucidity, whereas Lelouch wanders toward wish fulfillment.

Still, Lelouch the romantic-comic filmmaker retains some links to the New Wave. Whereas de Broca and Robert simply assume a comic, unalienated world, Lelouch attempts to justify and describe that world on many levels. Although the results are uneven, Lelouch deserves credit for stretching the limits of comic entertainment. Similarly, whereas the films of de Broca and Robert are thoroughly conventional in style, Lelouch's approach is much more experimental. These aspects of his work clearly relate to the New Wave's notion of the diversity and multiplicity of cinematic expression. Lelouch continues to follow the maxim that "one should put everything in a film."[15]

The concept of alienation provides an intriguing way of situating Lelouch in relation to other French filmmakers. Alienation is a major theme in Lelouch's work, especially in his early films. Like many of his contemporaries, Lelouch is strongly interested in how the changes and dislocations of the modern world have affected our lives. However, he is even more concerned with showing that an immanent happiness can overcome all obstacles. Thus, Lelouch's work can be connected to the optimistic comedies of de Broca, Robert, and Tacchella as well as to the alienation films of Godard and Resnais.

10
Conclusions

Claude Lelouch is in many ways a very modern filmmaker, an experimentalist shaping narrative cinema to his own personal vision. He shares with New Wave directors like Godard, Resnais, Truffaut, Varda, and Demy a commitment to the cinéma d'auteur and to cinema's multiple levels of communication. Stylistically, Lelouch's experimental approach can be summarized by six major points: (1) His sophisticated and emphatic visual style not only enhances the plot but also signifies in its own right. (2) He frequently uses complex narrative structures, including the interpenetration of past and present, the juxtaposition of parallel plots, and the building of ambiguities and enigmas. (3) His cinema is reflexive; it describes and comments on itself. (4) He mixes documentary techniques like hand held camerawork and semiimprovised acting with fictional structures. (5) He mixes a variety of genres: love story, adventure film, comedy, crime film, and historical film. (6) His use of music favors a freer, more contrapuntal relationship between music and image over the traditional idea of music as intensifier.

For what purpose does Lelouch employ these various techniques? Clearly, they have an analytic-critical function in his work, as in the films of Godard or Antonioni. They present a complex and ambiguous modern reality. The elaborate narratives of *Life, Love, Death, The Crook,* and *And Now My Love,* among others, reproduce a complex web of relationships around the characters. Devices such as subjective storytelling (*Live for Life, Life, Love, Death*) and the suppression of key information (*Life, Love, Death, The Crook*), indicate the ambiguity of experience. Visual style and music probe the multiple layers of experience, revealing subtleties beyond the main plot line. Reflexive devices question the nature of cinema itself, and the mixture of genres provides new forms and insights for popular myths.

This kind of filmmaking not only indicates modern complexity but also interprets it. Lelouch is to some extent a filmmaker who tries to understand his society actively, to suggest modes of action in a complex world. His characters must find their way through a fragmented and

146

ambiguous context. This aspect of Lelouch's work lies squarely within the experimental-critical tradition of the 1950s and 1960s.

The same innovative techniques also serve another, quite different function in Lelouch's fiilms. They present the look and feel of modernity for a lyrical purpose. Lelouch situates his films in the present by means of structure as well as content. But behind a surface complexity, he sees our world as quite simple, traditional, and comedic. Romantic love, individual adventure, and simple pleasure have all survived contemporary alienation; that, in a nutshell, is the message of most of Lelouch's films. Within this framework, the modernist techniques become a kind of lyrical game. Reality can be mastered, therefore the intricacies of modern life are ultimately comedic. Lelouch celebrates the marvelous variety of a world that still accommodates human needs. His complex narratives are puzzles to be solved by both the characters and the spectators. His visual style shows the richness of this world, and music suggests its emotional depth. His reflexive moments are in a sense "jokes"[1] because they point to the sheer joy of creativity in a lyrical universe.

The two attitudes, critical and celebratory, coexist in almost all of Lelouch's films. Generally, the comedic view wins out over a preliminary alienation. The pattern set by *A Man and a Woman*, where a crushing aloneness is transcended by love, has dominated Lelouch's work. He criticizes contemporary society mainly as a starting point, the beginning of a dialectic in which individual initiative triumphs over external and internal obstacles. A few films—*Une Fille et des fusils, Life, Love, Death,* and *Le Mariage*—end badly, which produces a sense of waste. A few others—the crime films from *The Crook* to *Happy New Year*—combine a joyous tone with the ironic awareness that individualism is becoming more and more unlikely. But the most characteristic Lelouch ending includes at least the possibility of happiness.

It is not easy to evaluate Lelouch's synthesis of critical and popular filmmaking. He cannot be dismissed for falling far short of the high standards of a Godard, because Lelouch is not trying to be solely a critical-intellectual filmmaker. Nor can Lelouch's weaknesses as a filmmaker of ideas be ignored because of his strengths in other areas. One must deal with the very mixed achievements of Lelouch's films, with the brilliant moments and the failures.

Certainly the guiding concept, the synthesis of the "festival film" and the "commercial film", is a fascinating and complex project. By combining these different styles of cinema, Lelouch attempts to communicate with the spectator on several levels. He does not succeed, though, in thoroughly working out his synthesis. In many of his films, a stunning overall design is sloppily realized. Lelouch suggests the examination of crucial and basic issues such as public vs. private life in *Live for Life*, justice in *Life, Love, Death*, history versus the individual in *And Now My Love*, and morality in *The Good and the Bad*, without ever really coming to grips with them. He seems to favor emotionalism over a penetrating, intellectual understanding. Lelouch's political ideas range from satiric and pithy *(Money, Money, Money)* to downright reactionary (some parts of *And Now My Love*) but he is most often vague and simplistic. Perhaps the end point of his films—the emotional fulfillment of love, friendship, work, and adventure—makes analysis less pressing. Why worry too much about the specifics of argument when one's goal is a mood, a feeling, a state of being?

The emphasis on improvisation in Lelouch's films can be seen in a similar light. Improvisation has many positive qualities, but it also tends to pull Lelouch away from from the hard, intellectual decisions that are part of filmmaking. He becomes an impressionist, wonderfully fresh and insightful in his best moments, and less successful as a director of ideas and structures. Improvisation works best at the level of feelings.

Though Lelouch has worked in various genres and under widely different conditions (low budget, high budget, filming in France, filming abroad), his films are substantially alike in tone, approach, and effect. To state this likeness very concisely, one could say that any Lelouch film elicits a mixture of exhilaration and disappointment. The artistic ambition, nimble wit, and stylistic virtuosity of his films are exhilarating, and they give a sense of cinema's enormous potential. But the muddy ideas and the lack of follow-through on a central design are disappointing and frustrating. They make Lelouch's films amusing rather than challenging, exciting but not passionately engaging. Some of the films are better than others, and the audience will vary, too. Some spectators may be thoroughly content with an original and amusing two hours at the movies, whereas others may be disturbed by Lelouch's sloppiness.

One should not conclude from this summary of the strengths and weaknesses of his films that Lelouch would be better off making simpler, less pretentious films. It is precisely the grandeur of Lelouch's vision that stimulates his experiments with visual style, narrative forms, and image/sound combinations. The subjectivity of *A Man and a Woman*, the intricacy of *The Crook*, the lyricism of *And Now My Love*, and the self-reference of *A nous deux* all start from the ambitious overall designs of the respective films. Without such stimulation, Lelouch's style would be empty and dull. So, his artistic ambition is not simply pretentious; it has created a number of wonderful moments and some very good films. Further, even his failures are often more interesting than others' successes. How many filmmakers would have attempted so daring and original a project as *And Now My Love*? Lelouch could use more discipline and a greater sense of how artistic and social aspects of a film intertwine, but these drawbacks should be balanced against the real virtues of his approach.

Claude Lelouch is now (in 1981) forty-three years old. Extremely precocious and productive, he has already directed more than twenty feature films. His work certainly has an internal coherence, and his best films—*A Man and a Woman, The Crook, Money, Money, Money, Happy New Year, And Now My Love, The Good and the Bad, A nous deux*—are impressive. However, Lelouch has rarely achieved a completely successful synthesis of entertainment and aesthetic-intellectual discovery. He is very good as a director of acting, images, and emotions, but less accomplished as a director of ideas and structures. Because of these flaws, Lelouch is not a great artist at the level of Bergman, Godard, or Truffaut. But his imagination, wit, spontaneity, and virtuosity make Lelouch an always fascinating film director.

Notes

Introduction

1. For an interesting discussion of film economics and audiences in this period, see Michael Pye and Linda Myles, *The Movie Brats* (New York: Holt, Rinehart and Winston, 1979, pp. 3–64. The one criticism I would make of their study of how economic conditions contributed to the success of young American directors, such as George Lucas and Francis Coppola, is that it ignores related (and earlier) developments in Europe.

2. Jean-Luc Godard, *Jean-Luc Godard par Jean-Luc Godard* (Paris: Pierre Belfond, 1968), p. 290.

3. Peter Lev, Interview with Claude Lelouch, August 23, 1977 (hereafter cited as Lelouch Interview, August 1977; see Appendix for a transcript of this interview). See also "*Si c'était à refaire,*" *Cinéma Français*, October 1976, p. 26.

4. Lelouch: "When I make a film I want to talk about all the things I love. I would like to talk about everything." Lelouch Interview, August 1977. Compare Godard's famous statement: "One should put everything in a film." *Godard par Godard*, p. 393.

5. James Monaco, *The New Wave* (New York: Oxford University Press, 1976), pp. 28, 118, 209–11.

Chapter 1: Beginnings

1. Michel Drucker, "Au Rendez-vous de Michel Drucker: Claude Lelouch," *Première* 1 (1976): 60, 62: Christine Gauthey, "Lelouch: On m'avait enterré trop vite!," *Le Journal du Dimanche*, January 25, 1976.

2. Léon Zitrone, "Claude Lelouch: Cent Mille Dollars en Trente Secondes," *Jours de France*, September 8, 1975, p. 40; "Claude Lelouch: Le cinéma, c'est ma vie, toute ma vie!," *Bonne Soirée*, September 12, 1971, p. 10; Sebastien Roullet, "Claude Lelouch: La vie, l'amour, la mort," *Télérama*, February 16, 1969, pp. 57–58.

3. Lelouch Interview, August 1977.

4. Guylaine Guidez, *Claude Lelouch*, Collection Cinéma d'Aujourd'hui (Paris: Seghers, 1972), p. 9.

5. Scopitone films have unfortunately disappeared with the machines that showed them. The following account is based on secondary sources. See, for example, Pierre-Richard Bré, "Sylvie," *Cahiers du Cinéma* 156 (June 1964): 45–46; Dujarric, Henriette, "Les Diffuseurs d'images," *Technicien du Film* 129 (July 1965): 8–9; Howard Junker, "New Perils Awaiting the Serious Drinker," *Film Comment* (Summer 1965): pp. 34–37; "Le scopitone est une exclusivité française," *La Technique Cinématographique* 263 (April 1965): 50–51.

6. Robert Benayoun, "Cinéma sur le zinc," *France-Observateur*, April 2, 1964, p. 17.

7. Lelouch Interview, August 1977.

8. Ibid.

9. Unfortunately the new ending is confusing, since we do not know if it is real or some sort of fantasy. Also, Pierre Barouh seems to have disappeared from this added scene.

10. Robert Chazal, "*Une Fille et des fusils*," *France-Soir*, June 4, 1965; Jean Rochereau, "*Une Fille et des fusils*," *La Croix*, June 11, 1965.

11. Lelouch Interview, August 1977.

Chapter 2: Subjectivity

1. "*L'Express* va plus loin avec Claude Lelouch," *L'Express*, January 3, 1972, p. 68. The "avance sur recettes" is a cash award given to promising screenplays to pay part of the production expenses. It is later repaid (if possible) from box office receipts.

2. Robert Franc, "L'homme à la Mustang," *L'Express*, December 12, 1966, p. 53.

3. Abe Greenberg, "Anouk Aimée Tells All!," *Hollywood Citizen-News*, March 23, 1967.

4. François Chevassu, "*Un Homme et une femme*," *Image et Son*, July 1966, p. 120.

5. Guy Allombert, "Cannes 1966: Lelouch l'admis," *Arts*, May 4, 1966, p. 55.

6. Peter Lev, "Claude Lelouch Discusses His Work, Francis Lai, Film Distribution, American History, and Justice," *Take One*, July–August, 1977, p. 19 (hereafter cited as Lelouch Interview, *Take One*).

7. Jean-Louis Trintignant, *Un Homme à sa fenêtre* (Paris: Jean-Claude Simoen, 1977), p. 84; Lelouch Interview, August 1977.

8. Jean-Louis Trintignant, "Mon premier film," *Le Nouvel Observateur*, February 2, 1966.

9. Jean-Louis Comolli, "Lelouch, ou la bonne conscience retrouvée," *Cahiers du Cinéma* 180 (July 1966): 68.

10. Trintignant, in his description of the film's production for *Le Nouvel Observateur*, describes the play of levels as "beautiful." Trintignant, "Mon premier film."

11. Similar scenes of isolation can be found in *Hiroshima mon amour*, *Breathless*, *Shoot the Piano Player*, and other important French films of the 1960s.

12. "Claude Lelouch: Je n'ai que trois thèmes—les seuls qui comptent—la vie, l'amour, la mort," *Le Figaro Littéraire*, February 10, 1969.

13. Lelouch Interview, August 1977.

14. Both Candice's monologue and "Les Ronds dans l'eau" have been omitted from the 16 mm print of *Live for Life* distributed in the United States.

15. Samuel Lachize, "*Vivre pour vivre*," *L'Humanité*, September 18, 1967.

16. Ibid.; R.S., "L'Objectivité du progressiste Lelouch," *Rivarol*, September 21, 1967.

17. A similar scene in Howard Hawks's *Hatari* (probably Lelouch's model here) is much more motivated: Capturing animals for zoos is the highly skilled and dangerous profession of Hawks's heroes. The chase scene is also the moment when the heroine proves herself to the Hawksian male group.

18. Albert Naud, *Tu ne tueras pas* (Paris: Editions Morgan, 1959).

19. Ibid., p. 7.

20. "Claude Lelouch et le succès," *Le Soir* (Brussels), March 3, 1967.

21. The film was based on real cases in France, Germany, and the United States. The courtroom scenes were shot at the Palais de Justice in Versailles, the prison scenes at the Maison Départementale in Nanterre (formerly a prison, now a shelter for the indigent). Many of the actors played themselves: the judge, the two lawyers, the prison chaplain.

D. L., "Avec Claude Lelouch, deux avocats (célèbres) assassinent . . . la peine capitale," *Cinémonde*, October 1, 1968, p. 29.

22. Gilbert Picard, "Lelouch a envoyé Amidou en prison," *Paris-Jour*, January 16, 1969, p. 17; Alain Spiraux, "Amidou a failli perdre la tête en jouant un condamné à mort," *Noir et Blanc*, February 20, 1969.

23. Pierre Montaigne, "Lelouch: une main tendue aux jeunes cinéastes," *Le Figaro Littéraire*, August 10, 1967.

24. Naud, *Tu ne tueras pas*, p. 114.

25. François Dhellemmes, *"Un Homme qui me plaît," Voix du Nord* (Lille), February 18, 1970.

26. Ibid. The statement Dhellemmes quotes from Lelouch sounds more like a publicity release than like an interview.

27. Jean Collet, *"La vie, l'amour, la mort," Etudes*, April 1969, p. 573.

Chapter 3: Collective Projects

1. Peter Lev, Interview with Claude Lelouch, December 1976. Lelouch's comments on *Far from Vietnam* were cut from the version of this interview published by *Take One*.

2. Lelouch Interview, August 1977.

3. Chris Marker is usually credited as the primary editor of *Far from Vietnam*.

4. Françoise Varenne, "Une comédie de moeurs et de caractère." *Le Figaro*, March 1, 1968; Guy Tesseire, "L'envers des jeux d'hiver de Grenoble," *L'Aurore*, March 7, 1968.

5. Judith Weiner, "Lelouch-Reichenbach: leur film sur les J.O. sera une histoire d'amour," *France-Soir*, February 21, 1968.

6. Pierre Billard, "L'Année Lelouch se présente bien," *L'Express*, March 25, 1968, p. 51.

Chapter 4: The Crime Film

1. Of course, friendship played a role in *Une Fille et des fusils* and *Les Grands Moments*, which are in some ways primitive versions of *The Crook* and the adventure films of the 1970s. However, *Une Fille et des fusils* stays at the level of adolescent games; it does not present mature heroes and adult friendships.

2. Lelouch Interview, August 1977.

3. Ibid.

4. The ambassador is Swiss just to emphasize that any country can be blackmailed.

5. "Un ministre, Jacques Duhamel, et la bande à Lelouch ont ouvert le Festival de Cannes," *France-Soir*, May 6, 1972.

6. André Halimi, "Claude Lelouch en question," *Pariscop*, January 13, 1971, p. 4.

7. Pierre Montaigne, "Un Drôle de prospectus inspire Lelouch," *Le Figaro*, October 29, 1971.

8. Or, as Lelouch says, "Comme ils bénéficient d'une santé folle . . ." "Claude Lelouch: Le cinéma, c'est ma vie," p. 10.

9. "Claude Lelouch: Je commence à faire du cinéma!," *Pariscop*, April 12, 1973, p. 6.

10. Ibid., p. 6; "Claude Lelouch et sa treizième film," *Le Figaro*, April 14, 1973.

11. Lelouch says that the opening citation was only a "joke." Lelouch Interview, August 1977. Still, other interpretations are possible.

12. Claude Lelouch, *La Bonne Année* (novelization), (Paris: Seghers, 1973), p. 57.

13. The crime film is a loosely defined genre concerned with crime, law enforcement, and punishment. The gangster film is a highly developed subgenre of the crime film. For one view of the crime film, see Stanley Solomon, *Beyond Formula* (New York: Harcourt Brace Jovanovich, 1976), pp. 157–98.

14. David Sterritt, "French Filmmaker Hopes to Make an Ideal Movie," *Christian Science Monitor*, August 7, 1978.

15. Lelouch Interview, August 1977.

Chapter 5: Un Chef d'Oeuvre Manqué

1. "Claude Lelouch: 'Un metteur en scène doit être en forme physique. C'est un métier de jeune,'" *Paris-Presse*, February 5, 1967.

2. "Claude Lelouch: 'Sur *Toute une Vie* je risque la baraque,'" *Le Film Français-La Cinématographie Française*, November 30, 1973.

3. Paul Wermus, "Lelouch s'allège de dix kilos et de trois milliards," *France-Soir*, November 29, 1973.

4. See, for example, Gérard Sire, "Claude Lelouch, une vocation de voyou," *Le Nouveau Cinémonde*, January 1971. Reprinted in Guidez, *Claude Lelouch*, pp. 149–53.

5. "Le combat de Lelouch," *Pariscop*, May 29, 1974, p. 5.

6. Compare Bertolucci's *1900* (1976), a leftist film, which stresses the roots and traditions of the peasantry and denies a viable tradition to the landowners.

7. Michel Delain, "Le siècle de Lelouch," *L'Express*, March 18, 1974, p. 50.

8. "Le combat de Lelouch," p. 5.

9. This interpretation suggested by Tania Zazulinsky.

10. Judith Crist, "*A Man and a Woman* on a higher plane," *New York*, March 24, 1975; A. H. Weiler, "Encore Lelouch," *New York Times*, March 22, 1975; Kevin Thomas, "Lelouch Touches All Phases in *Love*," Los Angeles Times, March 26, 1975; Mary Murphy, "New Critics' Unit Gives Award," *Los Angeles Times*, February 25, 1976.

Chapter 6: Moral Realism, Genre Optimism

1. Pierre Montaigne and Jean-Pierre Mogui, "Ce soir marions-nous," *Le Figaro*, December 31, 1974.

2. Christine Gauthey, "Lelouch: On m'avait enterré."

3. Ibid.

4. Andrew Sarris, "Lelouch and Lubitsch: One Ages Well, the Other Doesn't," *Village Voice*, May 18, 1978, p. 39.

5. A joke familiar from Jacques Tati's *Playtime* (1967).

6. "*Le Chat et la souris*," *Cinéma Français*, October 1975, p. 16.

7. Philippe Aziz, *Tu trahiras sans vergogne, histoire de deux "collabos" Bonny et Lafont* (Paris: Fayard, 1970).

8. Interview with Lelouch, *Le Journal du Dimanche*, November 22, 1970.

9. Micheline Deville, "Claude Lelouch: Les méchants sont toujours les autres," *Le Soir* (Marseilles), February 6, 1976.

10. Aziz, *Tu trahiras sans vergogne*, p. 65.

11. Curiously, the opening title is not on Lelouch's reference copy of *The Good and the Bad*. His assistant editor explained to me that it was added just before the film's release.

12. Nicole Jolivet, "Lelouch-Dutronc: On remet ça en août," *France-Soir*, January 24, 1976.

13. Lelouch Interview, August 1977.

14. Henri Béhar, "*Le Bon et les méchants*," *La Revue du Cinéma* 304 (March 1976):96–97.

15. "*Si c'était à refaire*," *Cinéma Français*, October 1976, p. 26.

16. Francis Esposito, "Claude Lelouch: 'Il faut décongestionner les acteurs,'" *Le Méridional* (Marseilles), November 2, 1976.

17. Ibid.

18. Ibid.

19. Lelouch Interview, *Take One*, p. 20.

20. Ibid., p. 20.

21. Ibid., p. 20.

22. Peter Lev, Interview with Claude Lelouch, December 1976. This sentence was cut (by *Take One*) from the published version of the interview. A similar statement is made in the opening narration of the film.

23. For anyone with socialist leanings, the Commune is a hopeful, positive moment in history. For Lelouch it is one more good reason to leave Europe.

24. Lelouch cuts away from this scene so quickly that we do not even know whether David has shot all the bandits or simply tied them up (the former seems more likely). The ellipse suggests that the violence is an exceptional, inexplicable episode in David's life, but it also makes the film more incoherent and it avoids the issue of when violence is justified.

25. Lelouch Interview, *Take One*, p. 18; Yonnick Flot, "Lelouch: L'Amérique c'est l'aventure," *Le Film Français*, September 19, 1973, p. 15.

Chapter 7: A Comedy and Crime Film

.1 "Claude Lelouch to Shoot Bankroll on his 'Ins and Outs,' 1937–80," *Variety*, January 30, 1980, p. 6.

2. This establishment has elements of both a traditional marriage bureau, where adults desiring a spouse are brought together, and the more modern computer dating service. It is probably closer to the former.

3. My remarks on *Robert et Robert*'s informal style are based purely on viewing the film, not on interviews or other material relating to its production.

Chapter 8: Lelouch and the New Wave

1. See, for example, James Monaco, *The New Wave* (New York: Oxford University Press, 1976); Annette Insdorf, *François Truffaut* (Boston: Twayne Publishers, 1978). For works defining the New Wave more broadly, see André S. Labarthe, *Essai sur le jeune cinéma français* (Paris: Terrain Vague, 1960); Raymond Durgnat, *Nouvelle Vague—The First Decade* (Loughton, Eng.: Motion Monographs, 1963); Roy Armes, *French Cinema Since 1946*, vol. 2 (Cranbury, N.J.: A. S. Barnes & Co., 1970).

2. Resnais was never a critic, but he was friendly with the staff of *Cahiers*. He

collaborated (as editor) on "Une Visite" (1955), a short 16 mm film by Truffaut and Rivette.

3. In some cases the very articulate *Cahiers* group stated and popularized ideas about authorship and style that were shared by many younger people in the French film-cultural community. They deserve credit for articulating and defending these ideas, but their work should not be viewed in isolation from the rest of the French film community.

4. See, for example, François Truffaut, "Le Cinéma français crève sous des fausses légendes," *Arts* 619 (May 15, 1957):1, 3–4.

5. Thomas Quinn Curtiss, "A Comeback for Love?," *New York Times*, March 2, 1967. I have paraphrased an awkward quote (probably awkward because of translation) from Lelouch.

6. See, for example, Jay Craven, "An Interview with Claude Lelouch," *Filmmakers Newsletter*, March 1974, p. 30, in which Lelouch says he improvised less on *Happy New Year* than on his earlier films.

7. See Dudley Andrew, *André Bazin* (New York: Oxford University Press, 1978), pp. 108–11. The description of Renoir's directing style—filming actors' responses like a documentarist, interest in the actor as a human being, fluid camera style, informality—sounds amazingly like Lelouch.

8. Jean Rouch, interviewed in G. Roy Levin, *Documentary Explorations* (Garden City, N.Y.: Doubleday & Company, 1971), pp. 135–37. Rouch, who has been making films since the late 1940s, also shares Lelouch's conviction that the director should hold the camera himself.

9. Craven, "Interview with Claude Lelouch," p. 30.

10. Lelouch Interview, August 1977.

11. Yvonne Baby, "'I wanted to treat *Shoot the Piano Player* like a tale by Perrault; an Interview with François Truffaut," *Le Monde*, November 24, 1960. Translated and reprinted in *Focus on "Shoot the Piano Player,"* ed. Leo Braudy (Englewood Cliffs, N.J.: Prentice-Hall, 1972), p. 23.

12. Lelouch Interview, August 1977.

13. Yonnick Flot, "Lelouch: L'Amérique c'est l'aventure," *Le Film Français*, September 19, 1973, p. 15.

Chapter 9: Alienation and Happiness

1. The ideas of mediating structure and megastructure come from Peter L. Berger, *Facing Up to Modernity* (New York: Basic Books, 1977), pp. 75, 130–41.

2. Henri Lefebvre, *Everyday Life in the Modern World*, trans. Sacha Rabinovitch (London: Allen Lane the Penguin Press, 1971), p. 94.

3. Quoted by John Ardagh, *The New French Revolution* (New York: Harper & Row, 1968), p. 406.

4. Kenneth Kenniston, *The Uncommitted* (New York: Harcourt, Brace and World, 1965), pp. 228–31.

5. Ardagh, *New French Revolution*, p. 345.

6. For example, the control of language in the New Novel, the intimate subject matter and emphasis on personal style in the New Wave. Jean Pivasset talks about filmmakers looking for a "voie propre" in cinema to compensate for political frustrations. Pivasset, *Essai sur la signification politique du cinéma* (Paris: Editions Cujas, 1971), p. 422.

7. Ibid., pp. 433–35. Pivasset distinguishes between the "Nouvelle Vague" of 1959-

61 and the "Jeune Cinéma" of 1963–68 (represented especially by Godard and Resnais). He finds that the more global lucidity of the second "movement" is itself a form of political action.

8. Susanne Langer, "The Comic Rhythm," in *Comedy: Meaning and Form*, ed. Robert W. Corrigan (San Francisco: Chandler Publishing Co., 1965), p. 124. Reprinted from Susanne Langer, *Feeling and Form* (New York: Charles Scribner's Sons, 1953).

9. Mary Blume, "Lelouch . . . Misunderstood Success," *Los Angeles Times*, August 11, 1968.

10. The films I have in mind are *Made in USA*, *Two or Three Things That I Know about Her*, *La Chinoise*, and *Weekend*, all by Godard, and *Blow-up*, by Antonioni. Another director using advertising-based styles in the 1960s to show both dynamism and superficiality in contemporary life is Richard Lester (*A Hard Day's Night*, *Help!*, *Petulia*).

11. Many of the best New Wave films (for example, *Hiroshima mon amour*, *Pierrot le fou*, *The Lovers*, *My Night at Maud's*) regard adults of twenty-five to forty-five as still young, still capable of change. Life need not end at twenty.

12. This is the kind of naive political argument to which the critics of magazines such as *Positif*, *Cinéma* (Paris) and *La Revue du Cinéma* object. See, for example, Alain Garrel, "A Propos de *Toute une Vie*, ou Lelouchiens si vous saviez", *La Revue du Cinéma* 292(January 1975): 27–40. The myth of America, land of gangsters, can also be interpreted more modestly as an implicit critique of sage and moderate France.

13. Annette Insdorf, "Why Americans Fall for French Film Romance," *New York Times*, September 9, 1979.

14. John Ardagh uses this term to describe the early films of Lelouch and Demy. *New French Revolution*, p. 412.

15. Jean-Luc Godard, *Jean-Luc Godard par Jean-Luc Godard* (Paris: Pierre Belfond, 1968), p. 393.

Chapter 10: Conclusions

1. See chapter 4, note 11, for Lelouch's comment on reflexivity as joke in relation to *Happy New Year*. See also Lelouch Interview.

Appendix

Interview with Claude Lelouch, August 23, 1977

(This interview was recorded in Claude Lelouch's office at Les Films 13 in Paris, France. It was conducted in French, and any awkwardness in translation is my responsibility.)

PL: Let's begin with *Le Propre de l'homme*.
CL: Yes.
PL: At the time of this film, were you in contact with or influenced by or inspired by the success of other directors, the young directors of the period?
CL: No, because when I made this film, first of all I had been making films for a long time, what you would call amateur cinema. So when the New Wave arrived in France—it arrived about '56, '56–'55, '56–'57—I was already a filmmaker at the time. I started when I was very, very, very, very young. I made my first films when I was fifteen years old, amateur films. So I was not influenced. I looked at their films, that interested me, excited me, but I have never been influenced by French cinema.

The cinema that always interested me the most was the American cinema. That's the only cinema that truly interests me. With all its defects, all the defects the American cinema has. Because for me, that's the most complete cinema and at the same time the cinema with the most defects. I've always thought that the Americans have wonderful qualities for cinema. They respect the public. They respect those who don't know the cinema. And I find that it's very important to respect people who don't have culture. In the world today there is too much of a tendency to have contempt for those who aren't cultured. Those who don't know things. But the American cinema respects those who don't know the cinema, so that an American film can be seen by someone who goes to the cinema for the first time. He can understand what happens, he can enjoy what happens, and I think that if there are people who aren't cultured, it's because of profound reasons.

Everyone wants to become cultured, everyone. Because everyone wants to learn things, and the structures, the means to do so, those who don't have the means. It happens that practically four-fifths are not cultured; one can say that in the entire world 80 per cent of the earth's inhabitants are without culture. I respect those who also think of that 80 per cent. I mean those who think that it's necessary to amuse, distract, and educate them. But, when Monsieur . . . Fellini makes a film, he thinks of the intellectuals.

PL: Not at the beginning, perhaps . . .

CL: Pretty much at the beginning, and today he thinks of the intellectuals, of those who have the opportunity to go to school. He thinks of those who have the opportunity to see all of his other films, he thinks of those who like a certain cinema, he doesn't think of the public. He doesn't think of those for whom the cinema is something essential.

PL: I think that that's a problem. The cinema is becoming a minority art today, television is becoming the majority art.

CL: Maybe, but what I like in the American cinema is that there's always been a relationship between the mass public and quality. And it's the only cinema in the world that offers, even in the largest, craziest superproduction, that makes an effort so that things are done with quality.

I've not yet seen, since I was born, a film that gives me, that leaves me with an imperishable memory. I've seen many, many films in which there are many sequences that interest me. But I haven't yet seen a film that pleases me from the beginning to the end. I saw such films, my great memories of cinema are from when I was very small, and I didn't know cinema at all. When I was very small, and I went to the cinema, for me it was fantastic. All the films were masterpieces, all of them. Even the lousy films. Because I didn't know the cinema, I took a total pleasure in seeing a film. I entered immediately into the story, I only concerned myself with the story. And the day that I began to understand cinema, the day that I became a professional, I gained in the professional sense, but I lost as a spectator. . . . And I take pleasure in cinema, because I remember being a spectator, therefore I think all the time of the public.

My dream would be one day to make a film that would be totally popular and at the same time of great quality. That I've never seen. I see either films of great quality or popular films, but rare, rare are the films where quality and generosity coexist. So I know that for me, for example, my ambition today in the cinema is to make one day, I don't know when, I don't know if I'm capable of it, a film of very, very great quality and at the same time of great openness to the public, therefore a film that's very, very "readable." That's my research, each of us has something, I mean that we all have a goal. But I know that if tomorrow morning someone asked me to make a festival film, uniquely for festivals, that's easy, that's too easy.

PL: Have you already done it?

CL: I don't know; *A Man and a Woman* has a Grand Prize from the Cannes Festival, so it's a festival film.

PL: But it's also something else.

CL: It's something else, you see, good. But if tomorrow morning someone asked me to do a festival film, I know that it's easy. If someone asked me to make a popular film, I know that it's easy. A big popular film, but I don't have the desire to make either one or the other. I don't want to. What interests me is to make a film that is of great quality and popular at the same time. To make a popular film is very easy, one uses things of an immense simplicity, so tomorrow morning if someone gave me lots of money to make a popular film, I'd refuse. And I know how to do it. If someone gave me lots of money to make a festival film I'd refuse, because I know how to do it. Besides, it might be easier to make a festival film than to make a popular film. But that doesn't interest me. What interests me is to make one day a beautiful, popular film, and that's complicated, because to find the synthesis between the noble and the generous. . . .

PL: I think that the problem of the public is fairly difficult in the cinema today. It may be more of a problem in France than in the U.S. One hears a lot about a crisis in French cinema. There aren't enough spectators, except for certain films.

CL: I don't think that there's a crisis. There have never been enough people who wanted to go see films, never. Never, never, never enough spectators. What's happening now is that people, for the moment, are mixing everything, television, cinema, audiovisual, they no longer know which way to go, but they adore cinema. The television programs that have the most success are films, so it's the cinema, they love cinema, they adore cinema, people adore the cinematic spectacle. The problem, I think, of cinema is that it's beginning, it's eighty years old. You know, painting: after eighty years of existence, nothing had been done. Literature: after eighty years of existence, nothing had been written. Music: after eighty years of existence, nothing had been written. So I think that cinema already in eighty years has succeeded in becoming the number-one popular art, which is already impressive.

But I think that now there will be a new generation of filmmakers who are young boys who were born in front of the television, who saw images and heard sounds before they learned to read and write, and who will be filmmakers, real filmmakers. At the moment, the cinema we see comes from literature and theater. There hasn't yet been a cinema of films, which comes from cinema. I mean which comes from that synthesis of sound and image. And I think that in coming years we will see great filmmakers.

PL: If we could go backwards a bit. . . . It seems that you don't have good memories of some of your early films, for example, *La Femme Spectacle,* which I saw a bad copy of in London.

CL: [Laughter.]

PL: Tania told me that it was not even one of your projects.

CL: No.

PL: It was a commissioned film. Who wrote the scenario?

CL: It was by Pierre Braunberger, the producer. I made this film for . . . a question of money, uniquely, it's a horrible film.

PL: It's the dialogue that's bad.

CL: Horrible. I haven't seen the English version but I've seen the French version. It's a horrible, horrible film. Very, very bad film. No, I've made some very bad films.

PL: And do you have good memories of the Scopitones?

CL: Yes, because that was amusing. Because it was a way to make money and it was . . . agreeable. When I made Scopitones I was surely preparing the musical comedy that I will make one day. For a long time I wanted to make a Western, starting from documents, from books, from ideas I had. [Lelouch is referring to *Another Man, Another Chance,* which he had just completed at this time.] But you know that I want to make a musical comedy. And that's thanks to Scopitones. That's thanks to Scopitones, which is going back fifteen years.

PL: One could say that some of your best films are already musical comedies—*And Now My Love, The Good and the Bad.* They have a mixture of music and . . .

CL: Yes, but that's not really a musical comedy. I know in my head what a musical comedy is and I know that in the next four or five years I will make a musical comedy . . . that's for sure. Because it's a dream. There are things like that. I wanted to make a musical comedy. Another project I'd want to make is a life of Napoleon. I've always wanted to very much.

PL: I was at the Invalides a few days ago. I'm beginning to get tired of French glory.

CL: No, for me it's a demystification. It's not at all polite to Napoleon.

You know, French glory, the French are . . . it's like everything. If you live with a woman you have to accept her completely, or reject her the same way. One can't take things halfway. I like Americans and I take them as they are, with all their defects. I like them anyway. The Americans also have many, many defects. But they have enormous qualities of generosity which make me feel good. But I feel good in all countries of the world. I don't know a country where I don't feel good. I adapt very easily to all situations. I can live with money, I can live without money, I can live in America, I can live in France, I could live in Russia. I have no problem of adaptation. I love, I am open to everything. I love cinema more than anything but I also love music, painting, literature. I love too many things, in life I love too, too, too many things, and when I make a film I want to talk about all the things I love. I would like to talk about everything.

You know, it's very difficult to talk about creation. Each time you talk with a creator, with an author, I don't think that you will one day get a precise response. Because he knows that he could tell you something else. Something very different. Because the mechanism of creation, it's a way . . . I think that creators are people who love life. If one is not seduced, curious, optimistic—each time that I'm unhappy, I can't write another word. Each time something is going badly in my life, I don't know anything any more. When I feel that things are going well, I can write kilometers and kilometers. So, each author has a system, and so you have other authors who will tell you, "Me, when things go well I can't write, and it's when things are very, very bad that I write." So, creation is something very, very, very, very particular for each of us. I know that I can't write unless an enormous number of things is going on, unless I'm enormously busy, unless I'm interested in many, many things. But one has to be curious. . . . One can't be afraid of being wrong. One can't be afraid of losing, one can't be afraid of being wrong.

You know, if I hadn't made some very bad films, I would be incapable of making others. I mean that I owe more to my bad films than to the others. I learned more from my catastrophes than from my successes. *La Femme Spectacle* taught me many things. *Le Propre de l'homme*, my first film. *Les Grands Moments*.

PL: Which is never shown.

CL: No, I had the negatives burned.

PL: Is that because after *A Man and a Woman* you didn't need this film? You know that the people who have seen this film like it a lot?

CL: What? *Les Grands Moments*?

PL: Yes.

CL: I know but . . . they're wrong. They're wrong, it's not a good film. It's not a good film because. . . . No, it's not a good film. Anyway, I don't feel, me, personally, that I made a good film.

PL: When you made your first films and also *A Man and a Woman*, you had a very small crew, didn't you?

CL: Very small.

PL: Five people?

CL: Six people.

PL: And that changed for *Live for Life* and the next films?

CL: I have a crew of about ten people—I mean ten, fifteen people— because . . . because one should keep people working and then because afterwards. . . . But I know that tomorrow morning I could make a film with five people, six people if I had to do it. But the ideal crew for me is fifteen people. Today the ideal crew is fifteen people, for the American film there were one hundred. . . . But it's not irritating.

PL: There are people who don't do anything, right?

CL: Some people who didn't do much.

PL: Can you tell me how *A Man and a Woman* was invited to Cannes?

CL: Well, by the most legal way. I presented the film to the selection committee in Paris, the committee for French selections, which chose the film. They said, "We're taking the film for Cannes," etc., etc. So, I went to the Cannes Festival and I won the Grand, and by the most legal means.

PL: It's a question that a foreigner would ask.

CL: Yes, it's completely legal and . . . I never tried to make combines for films.

PL: And how did you finance *A Man and a Woman* after *Les Grands Moments*?

CL: I financed it with . . . After *Les Grands Moments*, you know, I was in very, very bad shape, I had defaults coming. I had to pay all my debts in about six months. I said to myself, "If I can make a film in less than six months, write, shoot, edit, either I'll be in superbankruptcy or I'll save the company"—and that's what happened. With the money for my debts, the money I had to pay in six months, I made *A Man and a Woman*. *A Man and a Woman* did not cost much—$100,000—and I shot in three weeks. Anyway, that's very, very, very fast.

PL: Jean-Louis Trintignant says in his recent book that he suggested his character should be a race driver.

CL: Yes, the two of us talked about it. I saw at the beginning a lawyer and then, with Trintignant, Trintignant adores cars. We talked, and I said, "You know, it wouldn't bother me, if you want I'll make him a race driver, it's equally good." But I could very well have made him a lawyer. What interested me was not the man's profession, but the passion he had for his profession. In the film he would have been an impassioned lawyer. What interested me was to see—I've always been interested in my films to show that people have a job that they love, that passionately involves them. Because I like people who have a passion for their job. I find that the number-one diversion is work. That's why in all my films everyone has a precise job. There's never a main character without a precise job. I like people who work, because I find that wonderful.

PL: And for *Live for Life*, how did you make the Congo and Vietnam sequences?

CL: We reconstructed them.

PL: In France?

CL: We reconstructed them in Camargue.

PL: Both of them?

CL: Yes. We reconstructed that. We were set to shoot them in Vietnam. We were supposed to shoot the sequences in Vietnam, and then the insurance companies didn't want Yves Montand to shoot in Vietnam. Because of the insurance companies we were obliged to go to Camargue. But if not, normally we had planned everything to shoot them in Vietnam. I have filmed in Vietnam, anyway.

PL: For *Far from Vietnam?*

CL: For *Far from Vietnam*.

PL: You told me that you detest this film.

CL: I detest it.

PL: Is that because of the editing, or . . .

CL: No, it's because too many of us made it. And when there are several directors for a film, that's not good. It's fine for directors with the same tendencies to film together. For directors who are opposed to each other it's impossible to work together. I mean that politically we all had different ideas, technically. . . .

PL: Yet the film was well received.

CL: No.

PL: In the United States.

CL: Yes, but in the United States. . . . Me, I see, for example, most of the films that you don't like much in the United States are very well received in France, and most of the films that we don't like are very well received in the United States. That's because when we see things in France, it's as though they came from the planet Mars. And in France the critics rave about the American cinema. In your country there are many directors that are shit. Here they are national heroes. It's about the same here. I mean that . . . there are judgments that are completely false on all sides. It's difficult. It's very difficult for an American to judge a French film, it's very difficult for a Frenchman to judge an American film. It's very, very, very, very complicated. That's why I want to see how the Americans will react to my first American film, because I don't know how they'll take it. I know that it pleases the French . . . a big success in France. I don't know if it will please the Americans.

It's amazing how different languages and cultures can modify things. Make things either sublime or ridiculous. But the same conception, for example, you tell me when you went to the Invalides to see Napoleon, you saw that, as an American, as only ridiculous. Well, a Frenchman might not find it very intelligent, but it's a part . . .

PL: It's especially after two months in France, when one sees that all the time. It's not exotic, it's too much.

CL: No, but . . .

PL: That's why I came here to spend two months, because one can't talk about the French cinema without knowing France.

CL: That's very important because . . . France has very important economic problems, and even a political crisis, France is going to have a very important change of government. No, it's good that you come to see us close up. I think that . . . I adore these two countries. I adore America and France. Still, I have many different enemies. I have an enormous amount of enemies.

PL: Yes, it's difficult for me to understand the presentation of *And Now My Love* at Cannes. This film was voted the best film of the year in Los Angeles.

CL: When?

PL: 1975, by the critics' association of Los Angeles.

CL: I know, and at Cannes it was booed and hissed for two hours. So, I've said that I think that in France it's a political problem. I represent a political problem. Because my films have made money. Everything that makes money in France is very badly regarded. In France, if you want to be a hero, if you want to do anything, you can't make money. But it's not serious. I like these two countries a lot. I like them because, finally, one can do what one wants. I've never had a problem of censorship, I've never had a film banned.

PL: I've read that for *Une Fille et des fusils*, the ending would have been a bit different if not for censorship.

CL: No, no, it's me who wanted them all to die at the end, because I thought that it couldn't lead to anything else. To do what they did in the film cannot lead to anything else. I think that as soon as a young boy turns to stealing, his life can only be negative. I don't think that stealing can lead to anything positive. These young guys were so attractive to me that I preferred not to trap them. I preferred to kill them.

PL: But there are crooks—in the film *The Crook*, for example—who seem to escape.

CL: That's something else, because that's already a very important form of intelligence. Because the crook in *The Crook* is very intelligent. He's as intelligent as a political boss, as intelligent as a creator. . . . The result is terrible, but one needs the same intelligence to pull off a job like that as to be president of the Republic. In all those cases you need the same aptitudes. You need a spirit of synthesis. A spirit of synthesis, and I find that for me that's what intelligence is. It's the possibility of synthesizing things at all times. An intelligent person is a person who's aware of everything at every second. You say that today it's sunny, that's good, but only if there are many things around the sunshine that make it good. If you're on vacation, that's good, if you don't have very warm clothing, that's good, and the sunshine is good if other things cooperate. But what I like in people I consider intelligent is that they know how to be aware of an ensemble of things in making a decision, and not just one thing in particular. That's because life is made up of millions of things. The more one takes account of the ensemble of these things, the more one is able to do something. I know that when I make a film, if I do many things for the film, if I write the film, if I do the dialogue, if I'm the film's cameraman, if I direct, if I produce, it's because I'm a man of synthesis. I dominate things better if I do several things at once.

PL: There are several heroes who may or may not be truly bad in your films. In *The Crook, Money, Money, Money, The Good and the Bad*. For example, the character played by Dutronc in *The Good and the Bad*. For you, why does he join the Resistance?

CL: He joins the Resistance uniquely for personal reasons.

PL: For revenge.

CL: Very simply, to take revenge for the evil done to his wife. People are concerned with their own problems, and not with the problems of others. Politics is everybody's problem, and then there are personal problems. People put their personal problems in front of the problems of others. Dutronc in *The Good and the Bad*, he attacks the Germans because he doesn't like Germans. He attacks the Germans because the Germans hurt his wife. So, it's for personal reasons.

PL: That's why you put the citation at the beginning of the film. To show people that one shouldn't confuse a patriotic sentiment. . . .

CL: Absolutely. It's a film that is not at all patriotic. *The Good and the Bad* is the story of men who only think of themselves.

PL: When the film was shown in Los Angeles, it was very interesting for me to see that the Bruno Cremer character was booed when he received his medal.

CL: Bruno Cremer is truly bad. He's a truly bad man who thinks of himself and only of himself. What's the difference between a good and bad man? For me, a good man is one who thinks of others before thinking of himself. And . . . there are very few people who think of others before thinking of themselves. As soon as you think of yourself instead of thinking of others, it's suspect. But I think that we're all like that. We are all bastards, because we think of ourselves before thinking of others.

For example, show me a man who loves a woman, it's because he loves that woman more than he loves himself. I mean that we all love ourselves. I'm sure that you love yourself, I love myself, we all love ourselves, but if tomorrow morning you're able to love something more than yourself, now that's generosity. That's goodness. That's what makes a good or a bad person. For me. Because that's a personal definition. Every time that I've been in love with a woman, I know that I've loved her more than myself. I would do things for her I wouldn't do for myself. For me, that's the most important thing, to find someone one can love more than oneself. If it's a man or a woman worthy of friendship, worthy of love. Loving the other more than oneself, that's very good. That's a real generosity. That's very, very, very, very good.

PL: In *The Crook*, a film that I like, it seems that your style changes. This film is more ironic, more distant, and that continues in the films that follow. Do you feel there's a reason for the change?

CL: Yes. It's that in getting older one finds that things are less important. One takes less things seriously. It's probable that today I take less things seriously than I would have five or six years ago. I mean that today there are very few serious things. . . . Maybe it's for that reason. I don't see another reason. Perhaps in ten years I'll take nothing seriously. That's why I'm going to start making comedies. Because my state of mind is ready to make comedies. And I think that when one is very young, one takes everything seriously, one speaks seriously. But the great quality of age is precisely that it gives you a philosophy which takes things with much more humor. I mean that someone who ages well is someone who gains a sense of humor. In my opinion.

PL: And why did you give a big part to Charles Gérard, who was not an actor at the time?

CL: Because he had the ability to be a great comic actor in *Smic, Smac, Smoc*. Have you seen *Smic, Smac, Smoc*?

PL: Yes.

CL: He has a wonderful role, he is marvelous. I think that he's a good actor for playing a role, a precise role, always the same, whatever the film might be. In *The Crook*, in *Smic, Smac, Smoc*, and in *Happy New Year*, it's always the same role. He can't do anything else than what he is in real life. He is like that in real life.

PL: I wanted to ask you about *Smic* and *Money, Money, Money*. There's a very, very special comic sense in those two films, I think. I was hindered by watching those films here, alone in a room, because one likes to laugh with someone else. . . .

CL: Yes.

PL: . . . in watching those two films. So, I wanted to ask if you have any ideas on how to make that comic effect, which creates a sort of complicity between people.

CL: That's very important, laughter is something that one does with others. For example, this afternoon you will see my latest film, *Another Man, Another Chance*, and it's sad to watch this film all alone in a room. There will be three or four of you, and that's sad, because in my opinion you're going to see the film badly. You'll see it badly because this film was made to be seen with many people. With people who want to laugh and to cry.

For me, what interests me most in cinema is to make people laugh or cry, which are the two extremes. And . . . I find that a man who laughs or a man who cries is sincere. When one laughs, one can't cheat; when one cries, it's the same. One can cheat in the middle, between laughter and tears one can do whatever one wants. But, when a spectator laughs, it's spontaneous, it's true. Therefore, the whole world of cinema re-volves around either tears or laughter. That's what I like, to make people laugh or cry.

PL: It's very difficult to make people laugh.

CL: Not more difficult than to make them cry. Maybe it's more difficult to make them cry. I don't know, but they are both very difficult. But I'd say that these are the two things that interest me. They are the only things that passionately interest me, laughter and tears. I remember the most wonderful moments of my life, moments when I laughed with friends, or the days that I cried. The rest doesn't interest me. I remem-ber everything that made me laugh and everything that made me cry, but nothing else.

PL: *Happy New Year* begins with the end of *A Man and a Woman*. Is that for you a way of saying that something needs to be added to the earlier film?

CL: No, it's a joke. It's like in the film you'll see this afternoon, there are many points in common with *A Man and a Woman* . . . Clearly, it's intentional.

PL: With *Happy New Year* you use a very lightweight 35 mm camera for the first time. Does that have something to do with the very long takes you use in the films that follow?

CL: Yes, that's to say that from the moment I had this new camera to carry on my shoulder, with *Happy New Year* . . . I always dreamed of using very long takes. For me, the long take is the most beautiful thing in cinema, because one can't cheat. If one can't cheat, that's a very important unity of time, and the cinema in my view is that. You're going to see, for example, the film this afternoon has many long takes. For the race and a few other things, there's a little bit of montage, but I'm not in favor of montage. I'm not in favor because montage is trickery, it's lying. And with the long take I have the sentiment of being true, of being a little more true. Of approaching truth. And that's the most difficult cinema, one can't make a mistake. It's the length of the sequence shot that makes it the cinema I like best. You'll see my latest film, it's all in sequence shots.

PL: I think that there are still some resources in montage. For example, at the end of *Happy New Year*, where one sees first one character and then the other.

CL: Yes, it's an arm and one should use it. You'll see in my film, not everything is in long takes. There are scenes that are better served by montage. But for the scenes of emotion, the long take is stronger. At least, that's how I feel today. Perhaps in two years I'll say something else. Today I prefer to shoot in long takes.

PL: And with *And Now My love* you begin to talk about history, about the past. That continues with *Le Mariage* and *The Good and the Bad*.

CL: Yes. That's because now the past begins to interest me. It begins to interest me for reasons that I'm not able to analyze. I never know how to analyze. You know, if I didn't give interviews from time to time, I wouldn't know what I was doing. (Laughter.) I do things instinctively.

I never went to school. I never attended a film school. And when I went to school when I was little, it's as if I never went at all because I was very bad and I didn't listen. So, everything I know is what I've lived. There's nothing I know that I haven't lived. Afterwards, at the age of twenty-five, I started to read. I started to acquire culture at twenty-five.

PL: But you know cinema very well, perhaps as well as those who began as film critics.

CL: Because I've seen everything, everything. I know cinema because I've seen an average of two films per day for the last twenty years.

PL: That's the average?

CL: Yes, one could say that my culture is completely cinematographic. My culture is visual. I started reading at the age of twenty-five. Literature interested me at age twenty-five. Before the age of twenty-five only cinema interested me. All I saw was films, films, films, films and television. Literature didn't interest me at all. I'm more a man of images than a man of written words.

PL: It seems that you're not at all happy with the milieu in which films are made, so you put together projects like the Club 13 and the Club 13-Normandie. This is for what purpose?

[In the early 1970s Lelouch ran a film club, Club 13, for motion picture professionals in the basement of his production company. He presented a wide variety of films in evening and especially weekend screenings. A bar and restaurant were also available to Club 13 patrons. Lelouch ended the screenings after a few years, saying he had no desire to become a permanent cinémathèque.

The Club 13-Normandie, a small, private resort and meeting place for film people, opened near Deauville in 1977. It features a modern screening room and closed-circuit TV, plus a pool, sauna, tennis courts, and other facilities of a resort hotel.]

CL: It's for the purpose of modifying the relationships between all those who work in cinema. I would like the people who make films to see each other more often and attempt to talk. In cinema the most important part is the part that comes before the film. Before the camera starts. And before shooting a film, it's very important that the actors, the directors, the writers, the producers meet and talk in an agreaable environment, and try to talk, try to get acquainted. . . . Preparatory discussion is very important for everybody. So, I create places like that, for film people, they can come, the door is wide open. And I'm the first to take advantage. I meet many, many people before making a film.

First, before choosing actors, one must meet many, many, many. One should meet an enormous number of people if one wants to make a good film. Make a selection, take the best ones. But meeting people, you can't do that all the time in an office like this. An office is very . . . in general one is bothered by the telephone—not today because it's the month of August. There's no time to talk. So, I created a place for people where they don't have all these exterior things, where they're in a cloister, as if in a church, and they can meet, talk, tell stories. The Club 13-Normandie is that, and it's an enormous success.

I believe in knowing lots of people. I think that people don't talk enough among themselves, don't see each other enough, don't discuss enough among themselves. And that's all I'm trying to do.

PL: Do you have any precise projects for the Club 13-Normandie?

CL: For the Club 13, no, the continuous film screenings, I go every week, that's my role. No, my projects are first of all filmmaking projects.

PL: For example, I've heard that you were thinking of building a studio there.

CL: That's right. To construct very close by a studio for finishing films, that's to say editing rooms, mixing rooms, dubbing rooms, a place where one comes to finish the film. The filming will take place somewhere else. But I made a place for preparing films and finishing them. Preproduction and postproduction.

PL: Can you say a little bit about your next film?

CL: The next film will be called *Laurel and Hardy*. And . . . it's the story of two profoundly timid men. It's a film about timidity. It's the story of a fat guy and a skinny guy. Their friends call them Laurel and Hardy. It's a study, that's all, a study. And it's a film about timidity, and it's a comedy. The fat guy will be Jacques Villeret, and the skinny guy will be Rufus. (This film was eventually titled *Robert et Robert*, starring Jacques Villeret and Charles Denner as the two timid men.)

Filmography

1954. *Le Mal du siècle*. Short amateur film.

1956. *Une Ville pas comme les autres; U.S.A. en vrac; Quand le rideau se lève*. Short documentaries.

1957– Films for the Service Cinématographique des Armées.

1959. *Helicoptère SOS, La Guerre du silence*, etc.

1959. *Madame Conduit*. Short.

1960. *Le Propre de l'homme*. Screenplay: Claude Lelouch. Director: Claude Lelouch. Cinematography: Jean Boffety, Patrice Pouget. Cast: Claude Lelouch, Janine Magnan. Production: Films 13.

1961– Scopitones and commercials.
1964.

1962. *L'Amour avec des si*. Screenplay: Claude Lelouch. Director: Claude Lelouch. Cinematography: Jean Collomb. Music: Danyel Gérard. Cast: Guy Mairesse, Janine Magnan. Production: Films 13, Films de la Pléiade.

1963. *La Femme Spectacle*. Screenplay: Pierre Braunberger, Claude Lelouch. Director: Claude Lelouch. Cinematography: Patrice Pouget. Production: Films 13, Films de la Pléiade. Unreleased in France because of censorship problems. A dubbed, shortened version did play in Great Britain. British title: *Paris in the Raw*.

1964. *24 heures d'amant*. Short on the Le Mans auto race.

1964. *Une Fille et des fusils (To Be a Crook)*. Screenplay: Claude Lelouch, Pierre Uytterhoeven. Director: Claude Lelouch. Cinematography: Jean Collomb, Claude Lelouch. Music: Pierre Vassiliu. Cast: Amidou, Pierre Barouh, Jean-Pierre Kalfon, Jacques Portet, Janine Magnan. Production: Films 13, Films de la Pléiade.

1965. *Les Grands Moments*. Screenplay: Claude Lelouch. Director: Claude Lelouch. Cinematography: Jean Collomb, Claude Lelouch. Cast: Amidou, Pierre Barouh, Jean-Pierre Kalfon, Jacques Portet, Janine Magnan. Production: Films 13, Films de la Pléiade. Unreleased.

1965. *Jean-Paul Belmondo*. Short for Unifrance Film.

1965. *Pour un maillot jaune*. Short on the Tour de France bicycle race.

1966. *A Man and a Woman (Un Homme et une femme)*. Screenplay: Claude Lelouch, Pierre Uytterhoeven. Director: Claude Lelouch.

170

Cinematography: Jean Collomb, Patrice Pouget, Claude Lelouch. Music: Francis Lai. Lyrics: Pierre Barouh. Cast: Jean-Louis Trintignant, Anouk Aimée, Pierre Barouh, Antoine Sire, Souad Amidou. Production: Films 13, Films de la Pléiade.

1967.   *Live for Life (Vivre pour vivre)*. Screenplay: Claude Lelouch, Pierre Uytterhoeven. Director: Claude Lelouch. Cinematography: Jean Collomb, Patrice Pouget, Claude Lelouch. Music: Francis Lai. Cast: Yves Montand, Annie Girardot, Candice Bergen. Production: Films 13, Films Ariane, Artistes Associés (Paris office of United Artists).

1967.   *Far from Vietnam (Loin du Vietnam)*. Lelouch's footage of the American fleet in the Gulf of Tonkin begins and ends this collaborative project.

1968.   *Grenoble (13 Jours en France)*. Directors: Claude Lelouch, François Reichenbach. Cinematography: Claude Lelouch, François Reichenbach, Guy Gilles, Jean Collomb, Pierre Willemin, Willy Bogner, Jean-Paul Janssen, Jean-Pierre Janssen. Editing: Claude Lelouch, Claude Barrois. Music: Francis Lai. Lyrics: Pierre Barouh. Production: Films 13.

1968.   *Life, Love, Death (La Vie, l'amour, la mort)*. Screenplay: Claude Lelouch, Pierre Uytterhoeven. Director: Claude Lelouch. Cinematography: Jean Collomb, Claude Lelouch. Music: Francis Lai. Cast: Amidou, Caroline Cellier, Janine Magnan. Production: Films 13, Films Ariane, Artistes Associés.

1969.   *Une Homme qui me plaît (Love Is a Funny Thing)*. Screenplay: Claude Lelouch, Pierre Uytterhoeven. Director: Claude Lelouch. Cinematography: Jean Collomb, Claude Lelouch. Music: Francis Lai. Cast: Annie Girardot, Jean-Paul Belmondo, Marcel Bozzuffi. Production: Films 13, Films Ariane, Artistes Associés.

1970.   *The Crook (Le Voyou)*. Screenplay: Claude Lelouch, Claude Pinoteau, Pierre Uytterhoeven. Director: Claude Lelouch. Cinematography: Jean Collomb, Claude Lelouch. Music: Francis Lai. Cast: Jean-Louis Trintignant, Charles Gérard, Danièle Delorme, Christine Lelouch, Charles Denner, Judith Magre, Victor Upshaw. Production: Films 13, Films Ariane, Artistes Associés.

1971.   *Smic, Smac, Smoc*. Screenplay: Claude Lelouch. Director: Claude Lelouch. Cinematography: Jean Collomb, Claude Lelouch. Music: Francis Lai. Cast: Charles Gérard, Jean Collomb, Amidou, Catherine Allegret, Francis Lai. Production: Films 13.

1971.   *Iran*. Producer: Claude Lelouch. Direction and Cinematography: Claude Pinoteau, Claude Lelouch. A travel documentary with no dialogue or narration.

1972.   *Money, Money, Money (L'Aventure c'est l'aventure)*. Screenplay: Claude Lelouch, Pierre Uytterhoeven. Director: Claude Lelouch. Cinematography: Jean Collomb, Claude Lelouch. Music: Francis Lai. Cast: Lino Ventura, Jacques Brel, Charles Denner, Charles

Gérard, Aldo Maccione, Juan Buñuel. Production: Films 13, Films Ariane, Artistes Associés.

1972.   *Visions of 8*. A documentary by eight directors on the 1972 Summer Olympics at Munich. Lelouch's segment, "The Losers," shows the responses of defeated athletes.

1972.   *Un Après-Midi avec des motos*. Short documentary about auto and motorcycle racing.

1973.   *Happy New Year (La Bonne Année)*. Screenplay: Claude Lelouch. Director: Claude Lelouch. Cinematography: Jean Collomb, Claude Lelouch. Music: Francis Lai. Cast: Lino Ventura, Françoise Fabian, Charles Gérard. Production: Films 13, Rizzoli.

1974.   *And Now My Love (Toute une vie)*. Screenplay: Claude Lelouch, Pierre Uytterhoeven. Director: Claude Lelouch. Cinematography: Jean Collomb, Claude Lelouch. Music: Francis Lai, plus songs by Gilbert Bécaud, plus recordings of various French and American popular hits. Cast: Marthe Keller, André Dussolier, Charles Denner, Charles Gérard, Sam Letrone, Carla Gravina, Gilbert Bécaud. Production: Films 13, Rizzoli.

1974.   *Le Mariage*. Screenplay: Claude Lelouch, Pierre Uytterhoeven. Director: Claude Lelouch. Cinematography: Jean Collomb, Jacques Lefrançois, Claude Lelouch. Music: Francis Lai. Cast: Bulle Ogier, Rufus. Production: Films 13.

1975.   *Cat and Mouse (Le Chat et la souris)*. Screenplay: Claude Lelouch. Director: Claude Lelouch. Cinematography: Jean Collomb, Claude Lelouch. Music: Francis Lai. Cast: Serge Reggiani, Michèle Morgan, Philippe Léotard, Jean-Pierre Aumont, Christine Laurent, Valérie Lagrange, Michel Peyrelon. Production: Films 13.

1976.   *The Good and the Bad (Le Bon et les méchants)*. Screenplay: Claude Lelouch, Pierre Uytterhoeven. Director: Claude Lelouch. Cinematography: Jacques Lefrançois, Claude Lelouch. Music: Francis Lai. Cast: Jacques Dutronc, Jacques Villeret, Marlène Jobert, Bruno Cremer, Brigitte Fossey, Jean-Pierre Kalfon, Serge Reggiani. Production: Films 13.

1976.   *Si c'était à refaire (A Second Chance)*. Screenplay: Claude Lelouch. Director: Claude Lelouch. Cinematography: Jacques Lefrançois, Claude Lelouch. Music: Francis Lai. Cast: Catherine Deneuve, Anouk Aimée, Jean-Jacques Briot, Charles Denner, Francis Huster, Colette Baudot. Production: Films 13.

1976.   *Rendezvous*.
A nine-minute, one-take film with the camera mounted on a sports car moving through Paris at incredible speeds. It transposes the themes of daring and modern lyricism to a startling new context. Lelouch's best documentary.

1977.   *Another Man, Another Chance (Un Autre homme, une autre chance)*. Screenplay: Claude Lelouch. Director: Claude Lelouch. Cinematography: Jacques Lefrançois, Stanley Cortez, Claude Lelouch. Cast: James Caan, Genevieve Bujold, Francis Huster, Jennifer Warren, Susan Tyrrel, Jacques Villeret. Production: Films 13, United Artists.

1978.   *Robert et Robert*. Screenplay: Claude Lelouch. Director: Claude Lelouch. Cinematography: Jacques Lefrançois, Claude Lelouch. Music: Francis Lai, J. C. Nachon. Cast: Jacques Villeret, Charles Denner, Jean-Claude Brialy, Macha Méril, Régine. Production: Films 13.

1979.   *A nous deux*. Screenplay: Claude Lelouch. Director: Claude Lelouch. Cinematography: Bernard Zitzerman, Claude Lelouch. Music: Francis Lai. Cast: Catherine Deneuve, Jacques Dutronc, Jacques Villeret. Production: Films 13, Cinevideo.

1981.   *Les Uns et les autres (The Ins and the Outs)*. Screenplay: Claude Lelouch. Director: Claude Lelouch. Cinematography: Jean Boffety, Claude Lelouch. Music: Francis Lai, Michel Legrand. Choreography: Maurice Béjart. Cast: James Caan, Geraldine Chaplin, Robert Hossein, Nicole Garcia, Daniel Olbrychski, Jacques Villeret, Jorge Donn, Rita Poelvoorde, Macha Méril, Francis Huster, Raymond Pellegrin, Fanny Ardant. Production: Films 13, TF1 Films.

Bibliography

This bibliography includes those general works most frequently consulted plus a brief selection of the interviews, reviews, and articles concerning Lelouch in the specialized and popular press. Many additional sources are cited in footnotes.

"*L'Amour avec des si.*" *L'Avant-Scène du Cinéma* 58(April 1966): 67–70. Synopsis, reviews, photographs.

Ardagh, John. *The New French Revolution*. New York: Harper & Row, 1968.

Armes, Roy. *French Cinema since 1946*. Vol. 2: The Personal Style. 2nd enlarged ed. Cranbury, N.J.: A. S. Barnes, 1970.

Aziz, Philippe. *Tu trahiras sans vergogne, histoire de deux "collabos" Bonny et Lafont*. Paris: Fayard, 1970.

Béhar, Henri. "*Le Bon et les méchants.*" *La Revue du Cinéma* 304(March 1976): 96–97. Review.

Berger, Peter L. *Facing Up to Modernity*. New York: Basic Books, 1977.

Billard, Pierre. "L'Année Lelouch se présente bien." *L'Express*, March 25, 1968, pp. 51–52.

———. "Il y a Lelouch." *Le Journal du Dimanche*, January 25, 1976, p. 13. Review of *The Good and the Bad*.

———. "*Treize bougies pour Claude Lelouch.*" *Le Point*, April 9, 1973, pp. 74–75.

Chapier, Henry. "Annie Girardot et la nouvelle dimension lyrique de Claude Lelouch." *Combat*, September 15, 1967.

———. "*L'Aventure* de Claude Lelouch: une comédie sur la "connerie universelle."" *Combat*, May 5, 1972. Review.

———. "*La Bonne Année.*" *Combat*, April 19, 1973. Review.

———. "Plan explosif de Lelouch pour le "jeune cinéma."" *Combat*, October 10, 1967.

"Claude Lelouch: Je n'ai que trois thèmes—les seuls qui comptent—la vie, l'amour, la mort." *Le Figaro Littéraire*, February 10, 1969. Interview.

"Claude Lelouch: Le cinéma, c'est ma vie, toute ma vie!" *Bonne Soirée*, September 12, 1971, pp. 10–11. Interview.

Collet, Jean. *"La vie, l'amour, la mort."* *Etudes*, April 1969, pp. 572–74. Review.

"Le combat de Lelouch." *Pariscop*, May 29, 1974, p. 5. Describes the reception of *And Now My Love* at the Cannes Film Festival.

Comolli, Jean-Louis. "Lelouch, ou la bonne conscience retrouvée." *Cahiers du Cinéma* 180(July 1966): 67–68.

Cournot, Michel. "Au coeur du monde." *Le Nouvel Observateur*, September 11, 1967, pp. 40–41. Review of *Live for Life*.

———. "J'arrive juste!" *Le Nouvel Observateur*, June 10, 1965, p. 29. Interview.

———. "Lelouch la Honte." *Le Nouvel Observateur*, February 2, 1966, p. 36. Review of *Pour un maillot jaune* and *L'Amour avec des si*.

———. "Plus fort que la vie." *Le Nouvel Observateur*, May 11, 1966. Review of *A Man and a Woman*.

Craven, Jay. "An Interview with Claude Lelouch." *Filmmakers Newsletter*, March 1974, pp. 28–31.

Durgnat, Raymond. *"Paris in the Raw."* *Films and Filming*, May 1966, pp. 56–57. Review of *La Femme Spectacle*.

———. *"Vivre pour vivre."* *Films and Filming*, May 1968, pp. 25–26. Review.

Esposito, Francis. "Claude Lelouch: 'Il faut décongestionner les acteurs.'" *Le Méridional* (Marseilles), November 2, 1976. Interview.

"*L'Express* va plus loin avec Claude Lelouch." *L'Express*, January 3, 1972, pp. 64–70. Interview.

Eyles, Allen. *"And Now My Love."* *Focus on Film* 21(Summer 1975): 9–10. Review. Includes Lelouch filmography.

Flot, Yonnick, "Lelouch: L'Amérique c'est l'aventure." *Le Film Français*, September 19, 1973, p. 15. Interview.

Ford, Charles. *Histoire du Cinéma Français Contemporain, 1945–77*. Paris: Editions France-Empire, 1977.

Garel, Alain. "A propos de *Toute une Vie*, ou Lelouchiens si vous saviez." In two parts. *La Revue du Cinéma* 291(December 1974): 17–36, and 292(January 1975): 27–40. Extensive critical article.

Gauthey, Christine. "Lelouch: On m'avait enterré trop vite!" *Le Journal du Dimanche*, January 25, 1976. Interview.

Giammateo, Fernaldo di. "L'amore piccolo borghese." *Bianco e Nero*, June 1967, pp. 1–23. Scholarly article on *A Man and a Woman*.

Godard, Jean-Luc. *Jean-Luc Godard par Jean-Luc Godard*. Paris: Pierre Belfond, 1968.

Guidez, Guylaine. *Claude Lelouch*. Collection Cinéma d'Aujourd'hui. Paris: Seghers, 1972. Career study plus script extracts, interviews, reviews, bibliography, and filmography.

Insdorf, Annette. "Why Americans Fall for French Film Romance." *New York Times*, September 9, 1979.

Labarthe, André S. *Essai sur le jeune cinéma français*. Paris: Terrain Vague, 1960.

Labro, Philippe. "Savoir 'Voir' *Toute une Vie*." *Pariscop*, June 5, 1974, pp. 5–6.

Ledieu, Christian. "Claude Lelouch, cinéaste encore inconnu, est le recordman de sa génération." *Arts* 963(May 20, 1964): 2.

Lefebvre, Henri. *Everyday Life in the Modern World*. Trans. Sacha Rabinovitch. London: Allen Lane/Penguin Press, 1971.

Lelouch, Claude. *A Man and a Woman*. English translation and description of action by Nicholas Fry. Modern Film Scripts. New York: Simon and Schuster, 1971.

―――. *La Bonne Année*. Preface by Samuel Lachize. Paris: Seghers, 1973. Novelization of *Happy New Year*.

―――. "Lelouch: Impressionist with a Camera Brush." *Los Angeles Times*, December 17, 1967. Lelouch's theory of filmmaking as of 1967.

―――, and Uytterhoeven, Pierre. *Un Homme et une femme*. *L'Avant-Scène du Cinéma* 65, 1966. Script.

Lev, Peter. "Claude Lelouch discusses his work, Francis Lai, film distribution, American history and justice." *Take One*, July-August 1977, pp. 16–20. Referred to in the footnotes as "Lelouch Interview, *Take One*." This interview was conducted in December 1976.

―――. Interview with Claude Lelouch. August 23, 1977. Referred to in the footnotes as "Lelouch Interview, August 1977." See Appendix for a transcript of this interview.

Martin, Marcel. "Le bon et ses méchants." *Ecran* 45(March 1976): 9. Martin explains his dislike of Lelouch's films.

Monaco, James. *The New Wave*. New York: Oxford University Press, 1976.

Naud, Albert. *Tu ne tueras pas*. Paris: Editions Morgan, 1959.

Perisset, Maurice. "Le cas Lelouch." *Cinema* 9 no. 2, n.d., pp. 26–30. Defense of Lelouch against his critics.

Pivasset, Jean. *Essai sur la signification politique du cinéma*. Paris: Editions Cujas, 1971.

Roullet, Sebastien. "Claude Lelouch: La vie, l'amour, la mort." *Télérama*, February 16, 1969, pp. 57–58. Interview.

Trèves, Nicole. "The Slapsticks of Politics: Protagonists in French and American Films." *Canadian Review of American Studies* 5, no. 2(Fall 1974): 181–89. Compares *Money, Money, Money* to Woody Allen's *Bananas* and *Sleeper*.

Trintignant, Jean-Louis. "Mon premier film." *Le Nouvel Observateur*, February 2, 1966. On *A Man and a Woman*.

————. *Un Homme à sa fenêtre*, ed. Michel Boujut. Paris: Jean-Claude Simoen, 1977. An autobiography by means of interviews.

Zimmer, Christian. "Eloge de 'la Première Prise.'" *Les Temps Modernes* 304(November 1971): 754–62. Spontaneity in *Smic, Smac, Smoc, Petit à Petit*, and *The Honeymoon Killers*.

Index